W.E.B. DU BOIS

James Neyland

MELROSE SQUARE PUBLISHING COMPANY
LOS ANGELES, CALIFORNIA

Consulting Editor for Melrose Square
Raymond Friday Locke

Originally published by Holloway House, Los Angeles.

Cover Painting: Harry Ahn
Cover Design: Jefferson Hitchcock
Original Pen/Ink Drawings: Christopher De Gasperi

W.E.B.
DU BOIS

MELROSE SQUARE
BLACK AMERICAN
SERIES

CONTENTS

Chapter One

Conscience
on Trial

THE OLD MAN WAS accustomed to controversy; most of his life he had welcomed it, but this was different. He was eighty-three years old; he was ready to retire from the public arena, to rest on his laurels, preparing to settle down with a new wife and approach the end of life gracefully as the revered elder statesman of African-American causes. However, the United States government—his government, the system he had supported throughout his long life—was spitefully and maliciously attempting to discredit him and put him away in prison, where it could be sure

---

Though many people disagreed with W.E.B. Du Bois, he nonetheless was heralded as a spokesperson for his race because he voiced the thoughts and angers of his people.

of keeping him silent.

His name was William Edward Burghardt Du Bois, but most people knew him by the initials—W.E.B. Du Bois. He had been a spokesman for his race for over fifty years, a controversial one that not everyone agreed with, but respected as a man who had made people think, whites as well as blacks. Whether they agreed with him or not, people listened. That was why President Harry Truman, Secretary of State Dean Acheson, and Attorney General J. Howard McGrath had to silence him. Du Bois had become very vocal in support of peace at a time when the President was committing United States troops to a war in Korea.

The official charge against Du Bois was "failure to register as the agent of a foreign power." The indictment had been handed down on February 9, 1951, by a Washington, D.C., grand jury under instruction of Attorney General J. Howard McGrath. What Du Bois had done was to circulate a petition, known as the "Stockholm Appeal," asking all governments to ban the use of nuclear weapons. Since the United States was the only nation possessing nuclear capabilities at the time, this petition was looked upon as un-American.

Du Bois and virtually everyone in the United

States felt certain that he would be convicted and sent to prison, even though he and almost all knowledgeable people realized he was not a communist and not an agent of the Soviet Union. He was merely a liberal intellectual exercising his right to free speech.

But this was the 1950s, and a great many innocent people were being convicted for crimes of conscience.

Du Bois spent most of 1951 preparing for the trial. Five days after the indictment, he quietly married Shirley Graham in a private ceremony so that she would be able to come to see him in prison. It had been almost a full year since the death of his first wife, Nina, and they had been planning a wedding with all their friends, but cancelled it because of the urgency of the situation. The marriage to Nina had not been a happy one, and they had lived apart since 1934. Du Bois had met Shirley in 1936, when she was twenty-seven and he sixty-eight, and she had been his intellectual companion and confidante since.

On February 16, she accompanied him to Washington, where he and four other members of the Peace Information Center staff were arraigned. His trial date was set for April 2; the others would be tried later if he was found guilty. Du Bois asked for, and obtained, a delay until November 8 so that he could raise the money needed for his defense and so that his lawyers could prepare his case.

At this point Du Bois felt that his many friends and supporters would come to his aid. Plans were moving forward for his eighty-third-birthday party to be held at New York's Essex House on February 23 as a fund-raiser for the Council on African Affairs. However, the news reports of his indictment and arraignment quickly forced a change of plans. On February 19, the Essex House canceled the contract for use of the hotel, and organizers, who had mailed out the invitations in January, had to rush to find another site.

After being turned down by every hotel in New York, the hosts finally managed to obtain the use of Small's Paradise, a cabaret in Harlem, for the testimonial dinner that was to have three-hundred guests. A number of these guests suddenly canceled their plans to appear, and at the last minute three of the scheduled speakers backed out—Charlotte Hawkins Brown, Mordecai Johnson, and Rabbi Hillel Silver.

Already in despair over the indignity of being handcuffed, jailed, fingerprinted, and charged before avid newspaper reporters, Du Bois wanted to cancel the event, but Franklin

Paul Robeson, actor and political activist, supported Du Bois when he was charged with "failure to register as an agent of a foreign power," in spite of the stigma of association.

Frazier, the chairman insisted he go through with it. Other more courageous guests would be invited to replace the cancellations.

When Du Bois arrived at Small's Paradise, seven-hundred guests awaited him, daring the government witch-hunters to silence their free speech. Franklin Frazier, Paul Robeson, Herbert Aptheker, and Belford Lawson gave testimonials to Du Bois, which turned to a rousing demonstration for civil rights. Du Bois was gratified and encouraged by the support of people, many of them unknown to him personally.

During the months that followed, the man who had lived long enough to see himself become a legend among liberals and African-Americans would be heartened by similar unexpected support. However, it would not outweigh the betrayal that came from those he had known personally and worked with closely over the years. The greatest of these betrayals came from the NAACP, the National Association for the Advancement of Colored People, which he had helped found in 1909, and to which he had devoted twenty-eight years of his life. On March 12, 1951, the NAACP board voted not to aid Du Bois in his legal case, because it was "obvious he is being supported by the USSR." He had been judged guilty by his peers without trial.

Du Bois expected his defense and that of the other four indicted, without help from the NAACP, would cost between fifty-thousand and one-hundred-thousand dollars. He feared this amount would be impossible to raise, but he and Shirley set out to try by touring the country and setting up speaking engagements. They organized a central office for the defense fund in New York, with Paul Robeson and former Minnesota Governor Elmer Benson as co-chairmen and former schoolteacher Alice Citron as secretary. Citron had been fired in 1950 after eighteen years teaching school in New York because she refused to take a loyalty oath.

They began the tour in June, and the first speaking engagement was in Chicago, where they were able to obtain the Coliseum. Fifteen-thousand people showed up, contributed when the plate was passed, and cheered Du Bois' words.

The disappointment for Du Bois, in Chicago as in most of the country, was that his audiences were largely white. He understood the reasons few blacks were willing to attend; they were far more vulnerable to government persecution than whites. He had devoted most of his life to fighting their cause, and now as

President Harry S. Truman had committed troops to Korea, and anyone who was speaking "un-american," i.e., against the government's actions, was considered a threat to national

security. Du Bois, at the time, was circulating a petition known as the Stockholm Appeal, asking all governments to ban nuclear weapons. This was looked upon unfavorably in Washington.

the fight was nearing an end it would have been gratifying to know that his own people appreciated him.

In New York it was at first difficult to obtain an auditorium that would permit him to appear, but the National Council of the Arts, Sciences, and Professions, led by Alice Barrows, obtained Town Hall in September and drew an enthusiastic crowd. This organization came out early in support of Du Bois by issuing "A Statement to the American People" in June, signed by 220 leaders of the arts, sciences, and professions.

There were many other written statements of support from all over the world. The International Union of Students wrote a letter to the Department of Justice; an International Committee in Defense of Dr. W.E.B. Du Bois and His Colleagues was formed, producing a petition signed by hundreds of college professors from all over the world; and other messages came from the International Federation of Teachers' Unions, the International Federation of Women, and the World Federation of Scientific Workers. Some offered funds, but all were turned down because of the charges that Du Bois and his associates were "agents of a foreign power." Money for their defense had to come only from the United

States.

Eventually about $35,000 was raised, and it proved to be sufficient, especially when attorney Vito Marcantonio offered to handle Du Bois' legal defense without a fee, which would have been about $10,000. (The previous year, Du Bois had attempted to help out Marcantonio's campaign for congress by appearing on the American Labor Party ticket with him as a candidate for the Senate.)

On November 8, 1951, Du Bois went to Washington and surrendered himself to the authorities for trial. He was again handcuffed, jailed, and led into the courtroom as a prisoner. The man whose dark brown skin had once had a luminous glow even in old age now looked pale and drawn. Lines had developed around his dark, intense eyes from the strain, and he appeared small and tired and old. He was now completely bald, and his mustache and Van Dyke beard were entirely white.

Federal Judge Matthew F. McGuire was to hear the case, and Assistant Attorney General Maddrix represented the Justice Department for the prosecution, with Vito Marcantonio handling the defense. The jury selected consisted of eight blacks and four whites. The case for the prosecution rested primarily on the testimony of O. John Rogge, a former U.S.

Assistant Attorney General who had been involved in the Peace Information Center as well as with the World Congress of the Defenders of Peace, the latter being the organization that was alleged to be an agency of the Soviet Union and formally tied to the former.

To everyone's astonishment, Rogge completely fell apart on the stand. He became so flustered and unsure of himself that he was even unable to identify his close associate W.E.B. Du Bois sitting in the defendant's chair until Du Bois voluntarily stood up "to help him out."

As Rogge's testimony unfolded, it quickly became evident that the prosecution had absolutely no case; all they had was the "opinion" of Rogge that the two organizations, as well as the Stockholm Appeal, were engaged in activities favored by the Soviet Union. He admitted to being an agent of a foreign power himself, but that country was Yugoslavia not the Soviet Union. He had visited the Soviet Union, but had no discussions with any Russian officials concerning these matters.

The judge realized that the Department of Justice had hoped to try this case in the press, with so much publicity that it would not have to present a real case to a prejudiced jury.

After five days of listening to the prosecution, without even beginning to hear Marcantonio's defense, Judge McGuire dismissed the jury and entered a verdict of acquittal, stating: "The Government has alleged that Peace Information Center was the agent of a foreign principal. They proved the existence, in my judgment, of the Peace Information Center. They certainly proved the existence of the World Council for Peace.... There may have been, and I take it as proven, there were individuals who were officers of both; but...in this case the Government has failed to support, on the evidence adduced, the allegations laid down in the indictment."

It was a surprise to everyone in the courtroom, prosecution and defense alike. Du Bois sat stunned in silence. Shirley fainted. And Judge McGuire, sensing applause was about to break out, demanded no demonstration of any kind.

For Du Bois, this was a bittersweet victory. It was sweet to know that he had won and that the Attorney General's office was made to look the fool it was. But a sense of bitterness lingered, because he had been betrayed on virtually all sides, and in the twilight of his life almost a full year had been taken from him by a government he had trusted.

Chapter Two

A Special Child

THE YEAR 1868 WAS a very important one in African-American history. Not as dramatic as 1865, when blacks were freed from slavery at the close of the Civil War, 1868 was the year when many of the rights and privileges of citizenship were realized in the period known as Reconstruction. In many parts of the United States, it was the first year that African-Americans were permitted to vote, and it was the year that the Freedmen's Bureau, after a slow start, managed to establish schools to begin educating the former slaves.

Du Bois' mother, Mary Burghardt, came from a strict and hardworking New England family. "She was rather silent, but determined and very patient," he wrote of her later.

For the newly enfranchised U.S. citizens, it was a time of great hope and expectation. The future looked bright, and it was bolstered by a Fourteenth Amendment to the Constitution.

It was in this year, on February 23, that a child was born in a five-room clapboard house on Church Street in Great Barrington, Massachusetts, who would grow up to be one of the most controversial leaders in African-American history. He was given the name William Edward Burghardt Du Bois (pronounced "Du Boyce"), and he grew up with more privileges and advantages than most blacks in the United States experienced at the time. Some have even said that he was spoiled. He experienced very little racial prejudice in his formative years, and he certainly knew nothing of the hardships of slavery, which continued to affect many African-Americans long after the institution had been abolished.

In his adult years, Du Bois always referred to his childhood as "idyllic." However, it does not seem possible that he could have escaped some form of racial prejudice, even in Massachusetts, and one cannot help but wonder if he did not use this term relatively, in comparison to the difficulties experienced by his contemporaries. It is true that his circumstances and family background were considerably different from almost anyone else of his time. At this point, few black families in the United States had passed through several generations of freedom, and almost none could trace their heritage as could the Burghardt and Du Bois families.

Of the two, it was the Burghardts who had the greatest effect on the young Du Bois. They had lived in that area of western Massachusetts and the Hudson Valley for over a hundred years, since their earliest known ancestor, Tom, had been brought there by Dutch slave traders and sold to the white Burghardts. Tom had been freed by service in the Revolutionary War, as a private in Captain John Spoors Company, Colonel John Ashley's regiment.

Tom's son Jack, who was involved in Shay's Rebellion, married twice; by his second wife Violet, he had six children, the youngest of whom, Othello, married Sally, and they produced a very large family. Othello and Sally Burghardt, the grandparents of W.E.B. Du Bois, were third generation New Englanders as well as third generation freedmen, and they appear to have been as rigidly puritanical as their white neighbors. They also seem to have possessed some degree of snobbishness as well.

They did not consider any man good enough to marry their youngest daughter, Mary Sylvina, who made at least two attempts to avoid growing old as a spinster. At age thirty, she had an affair with a first cousin, John Burghardt, by whom she had an illegitimate son named Idelbert. Five years later, in 1867, she met Alfred Du Bois, a handsome newcomer to Great Barrington, and she had to run away to Housatonic to marry him against her parents' wishes. Even then the Burghardts were determined to break up the marriage.

Alfred Du Bois was light-skinned enough to pass as white, but he chose not to do so. He was born in Haiti in 1825, to Alexander Du Bois, a mulatto, and an unknown woman. Little is known of the Du Bois black heritage, though the white lineage in America originates with Jacques Du Bois who emigrated from Flanders in the early seventeenth century and settled in Ulster County, New York. Alfred's grandfather, Dr. James Du Bois, was a loyalist in the Revolutionary War and found it more comfortable to leave the country after ending up on the losing side. Granted lands in the Bahamas, he moved there. James had two sons by a black woman, Alexander and John, both of whom were white enough to

In this drawing, Mary Burghardt Du Bois holds her newborn son, William, who was born on February 23, 1868 in a small house on Church Street in Great Barrington, Massachusetts.

"pass," so he sent them to school in Connecticut.

When James died, his sons were removed from school by their white relatives and cast out on their own. For awhile, Alexander lived in Haiti, where his son Alfred was born, then returned to the United States, opening a grocery store in New Haven, Connecticut.

When the Civil War began, Alfred was thirty-six, and he joined the Union Army as a private, serving throughout the conflict. Two years later, he arrived in Great Barrington, met Mary Sylvina Burghardt, and after a whirlwind courtship, married her.

It seems likely that the newlyweds expected the Burghardts to give in eventually and accept the marriage, for they chose to settle in Great Barrington, renting a house on Church Street belonging to Jefferson McKinley, a freedman from South Carolina. But Mary's parents were stubborn, even after she became pregnant; they would not accept her husband under any circumstances.

In 1868, after the birth of their son William, the couple agreed that the only way their marriage could survive would be for them to move away from Mary's parents. It was probably the right decision, but they made one mistake; while Alfred went to New Milford,

Du Bois' father, Alfred, was a poetic type who loved to travel. He served in the Union Army, met Mary in 1867 and married her soon afterwards over the protests of her family.

Connecticut, to get work and set up a home for his wife and child, they would stay with her parents at the Burghardt farm outside town. When the time came for Mary and the baby to join Alfred, the Burghardts would not allow it.

It is not known what sort of pressure Othello and Sally Burghardt applied to keep Mary with them, for she might have simply run away as she did when she was married. Alfred persisted in his efforts to hold onto his family for almost a year, then finally gave up. As far as William knew, he was never heard from again. However, some contact was maintained with Alfred's father, Alexander Du Bois, who had settled in New Bedford, Massachusetts, for young William would go to meet him when he was fifteen.

Under the influence of his grandparents, William was pampered, even spoiled. Othello was rather austere and quiet, spending most of his time sitting in a high-backed chair by the fireside because of a bad hip. Grandmother Sally was apparently the real force in the family, constantly working and managing the farm and household. Because Mary was the youngest of about a dozen children, William had numerous aunts and uncles who would appear from time to time, with cousins of various ages. His uncle Jim was the closest in age to his mother, and he also appears to have maintained the closest ties, though William later recalled fond memories of his aunts Lucinda Gardner Jackson and Minerva Newport.

Those early years on the farm were probably as idyllic for a young boy as William remembered them. It was an insulated world, held in on itself by the mountains around. However, it was as insular as it was insulated. The Burghardts' New England reserve included suspicion or distrust of outsiders; William was brought up to value the "old families" and to look down on new settlers or summer residents who came in from the cities. With their New England upbringing, the Burghardts taught William as a child that "cleanliness was next to godliness," and they always saw to it that he dressed well. One photograph taken of him shortly before starting to school shows him outdoing "Little Lord Fauntleroy," wearing velvet knee-breeches, white stockings, patent-leather slippers, and a ruffled collar, with his long hair forced into ringlets.

Among the values the Burghardts instilled in William was a belief in the importance of education. It was so important that, in 1873, when William was five years old, Mary was permitted to move back to the town of Great

W.E.B. Du Bois and his first wife, Nina, and their young son, Burghardt Gomer. The family moved to Atlanta soon after the baby's birth where Du Bois became an instructor at Atlanta

University, charged with setting up the school's "Negro Problem" program. Nina was glad to leave the slums of Philadelphia where they had been living.

Barrington so that her son could attend school. She found rooms for the two of them above the stables on the Sumner estate, which was next door to the school, and she obtained day work cleaning houses.

William's first teacher at school was Miss Cross. Almost immediately she perceived that he was a bright child who was willing to apply himself to his studies, and he became a favorite of hers. Even in these early years in school William faced no color barriers. Only about one percent of Great Barrington's population of about five-thousand was of African-American descent, a very small minority, but William was welcomed as a friend by his fellow students, virtually all of them white.

He was fully aware that he and his mother were poor, and there is some indication that he may have felt some embarrassment that his mother cleaned other people's houses, but William bridged any gap there might have been through his intelligence and his personality. However, this was not the case with those who were less fortunate than he was. Because of the Burghardts' emphasis upon the importance of being "old family," he looked down on the children of the Irish and German immigrants who worked in the local factories. Some who knew him at this time considered

As a youngster, Du Bois had already taken on a snobbish appearance. In this photograph he is dressed replete with velvet knee-breeches, white stockings and patent-leather slippers.

him a snob.

When William was twelve, his mother suffered a stroke, which caused some paralysis of her left side, yet she continued to do her work so that her son could go on to high school, which he entered the following year. It was probably because of Mary's difficulty climbing stairs that they moved to a one-story house near the train station, and William obtained his first job in order to help out with the expenses. That job was the task of filling the coal stove for Madame L'Hommedieu each day. In order to supplement their income further, he added the job of selling newspapers after school and on Saturdays, then took on representing the A&P Company locally, which at the time sold tea through commission salesmen, a concept that later grew to the grocery chain.

But even at this young age, William was ambitious for less menial and more intellectual pursuits. By the time he was fifteen, now acquiring a degree of racial consciousness, he managed to work his newspaper sales job into a position as local correspondent for a black newspaper, the *New York Globe,* as well as for the *Springfield Republican.*

In his later writings, Du Bois had little to say about his feelings or about the way others felt toward him when he was young. He did say that he was admired by his fellow students for his ability to excel scholastically, which was probably true to some extent. But this view of how he was viewed appears to have been colored somewhat by his own pride at knowing he was the best. Invariably he won high-school debates by "his overpowering manner," which is how some later described him. Others, including some of his teachers, considered him "conceited" and "a spoiled child." Yet all respected his intelligence and his drive to learn.

To try to understand the adolescent W.E.B. Du Bois, one can only turn to conjecture. However, he has given one clue to understanding in a comment he later made about the only other black student in his high school; he admitted that he was "ashamed" of him because he "did not excel" and dropped out of school before graduation. This suggests that, despite the fact that he was accepted socially by his peers, he had become somewhat sensitive about the color of his skin and about the way African-Americans were viewed generally by the white population. Whether it was true or not, he must have felt he had to prove himself by excelling. And from this could have come much of his enormous drive.

Du Bois was born in this five bedroom clapboard house in Great Barrington, Massachusetts. Although Mary's parents were well-to-do, she and her husband lived here near poverty, by whatever

It was during his high-school years that he later recalled his first experience with racial discrimination. In the nineteenth century, in polite society, it was the custom to exchange calling cards, *cartes d'visite,* among social equals, especially when meeting someone for the first time. (We still follow this practice on a business level.) Although summer residents were not fully welcomed by the Great Barrington natives, who maintained their New England restraint, fifteen-year-old William offered his card to a young white girl who was there for the season, and she refused it.

means they could. Alfred soon grew tired of these conditions and went to New Milford, Connecticut to seek a better life for his wife and family.

The girl may or may not have made it clear that he was unacceptable because of his color; whatever the case, William understood that it was because he was black, and he never forgot the slight.

That summer was significant for him in one other way. It proved to be the one and only time he would see his paternal grandfather, Alexander Du Bois. His mother permitted him to travel to New Bedford to see the old man. Her own parents, Oliver and Sally Burghardt, were now dead, and Mary may have had some sense that, because of her stroke, her own life could not last much longer. When she was gone, William would have no immediate family left, only aunts and uncles and cousins.

It was Alexander's third wife, Anna Green, who extended the invitation for the visit, and Mary saved up the funds for the railroad trip for her son. What struck William most strongly about the visit was the formality and ceremony of his grandfather's lifestyle, which contrasted strongly with the casual country ways of Great Barrington. Later he described Alexander as austere, "set in his ways, proud and bitter." He also commented that he felt he was an embarrassment to his grandfather because of his darker color. However, that may have been merely the sensitivity of an adolescent who was rapidly developing an inferiority complex the more he ventured out into the world, a complex he felt he had to overcome by excelling.

In the spring of 1884, at the age of sixteen, William graduated from Great Barrington High School. He was the only black student in the class of twelve. He was also the valedictorian and the only member of the class who would go on to college, though not for over a year and not to the college he wanted.

He had managed to get through high school because the public schools were free. A college education cost money. Not only did Mary Du Bois have to work hard for low pay, which meant it was difficult to save, but her health was growing worse. In the summer after graduation, William obtained a job as timekeeper for the contractors who were building the Hopkins mansion in Great Barrington. The salary was one dollar a day, and he acquired the position through his friendship with Mrs. Hopkins' steward, Dennis, a mulatto.

The Burghardts claimed that the impressive mansion was being constructed with uncle Tom Burghardt's unpaid salary. Years before, Miss Anastasia Kellogg, who lived on Main Street in Great Barrington, had employed Tom but instead of paying him had held onto her money as a nest-egg for marrying well. She married Mark Hopkins, who took her money, invested it in building the Union Pacific, and made a fortune. Now she was using that money to build a mansion in her old hometown.

At one dollar a day, it was difficult for William to build up the nest-egg he needed to start college. He had his sights set on Harvard, which would be very expensive if he could not get some sort of scholarship. His high school principal, Frank Hosmer, pointed out

Booker T. Washington, educator, founder and builder of Tuskegee Institute in Alabama, was to be Du Bois' friend then nemesis as their political paths paralleled throughout their lives.

an additional problem for him; his public-school education was inadequate preparation for Harvard's high standards. Hosmer advised him to set his sights lower, at least temporarily.

Hosmer believed strongly in Du Bois' potential, and he worked to try to come up with funding for a scholarship to help pay for college. He joined with Edward Van Lennep, who was principal of a private school in Great Barrington, and Congregational minister, Reverend C.C. Painter, to put together the needed funds. It was Painter who came through with their $200 goal, obtaining pledges of $25 each from four congregations, his present one in Great Barrington and the three previous churches he had served as minister.

In 1885, Mary Burghardt Du Bois died. William was clearly devastated by the loss, but he continued to work toward his dream. He moved in with his aunt, Minerva Newport, and paid her for room and board.

By the fall of 1885, he was able to set off to college, not to Harvard but to Fisk University in Nashville, Tennessee.

In 1884, Du Bois graduated from Great Barrington High School at the age of sixteen (Du Bois at far left, back row). Although not well liked by most of the students, he was well respected

because of his intelligence his passion in his beliefs. He was the only black to graduate in his class, and the only person to go on to college.

Chapter Three

Drive
to Excel

SEVENTEEN-YEAR-OLD W.E.B. Du Bois had mixed feelings about going to college in the South. He desperately wanted a college education, but his pride—and that of his Burghardt relatives—demanded only the best, if not Harvard then Yale or Williams. He was grateful to Hosmer, Van Lennep, and Painter for providing him with the scholarship, but he was also resentful that they were trying to dictate where he would go to school.

The three educated adults thought they knew what was best for him. Although brilliant, Du Bois was spoiled by his family; he

At seventeen, Du Bois now had to find a college to attend. His relatives wanted him to go to the south so he could learn about southern Negroes but Du Bois found their advice insulting.

was a social and intellectual snob who thought the world revolved around New England. He needed to get away from his insular surroundings to see what the rest of the world was like. He needed to learn about the difficulties that African-Americans faced in other parts of the country, especially the South.

They attempted to explain their reasons to Du Bois, but he took offense that these white adults were attempting to tell him that he needed to learn about the black race. Objectively, they were probably right, but the young student only saw the situation subjectively, and it would be the subjective feelings that would mold the man.

Of the three who were attempting to guide Du Bois, Reverend Painter's views carried the most weight because he was providing the funds, and he was guided by a Christian missionary zeal, believing that talented African-Americans needed to be educated in order to help lift up others of their race. This and Christian charity were the basis of his appeal in raising the funds for the scholarship. The proud seventeen-year-old resented both, and his resentment began to turn him away from organized Christian religion.

In September 1885, when he arrived at Fisk University, Du Bois experienced serious culture shock. Although he must surely have heard about conditions in the South, he was not prepared for what he saw and faced in Tennessee. Although intellectually far ahead of most of his fellow students at Fisk, his sheltered smalltown New England background had caused him to be naive and innocent about life itself. At seventeen, he was one of the youngest students enrolled, yet because of his educational background he was permitted to enter at the sophomore level.

The adjustment must have been extremely difficult for him. He later admitted that he knew nothing about sex at the time, not even the basic anatomical differences between males and females. In his first few days at Fisk, he met a young woman named Lena Calhoun (the great aunt of Lena Horne), whom he considered the most beautiful woman he had ever seen, and he became infatuated with her but did not even know how to express his romantic feelings.

His adjustment was complicated by having been at Fisk less than a month when he contracted typhoid fever and came very close to not surviving. By the time he returned to classes in November, all the students and teachers knew who he was, and they welcomed him warmly with expressions of concern.

This immediate popularity set him apart even more as a very special person. From earliest childhood, much had been expected of him, and he expected even more of himself. He had always excelled, always been the very best at everything he undertook, so it came as a shock to him when, in November, he placed second in his English examination, and what was worse as far as his self-image was concerned, second to a white female. His competitive spirit was challenged by the fact that many of the female students did so well; he had been brought up to believe that men were naturally brighter and better than women, and it was difficult to adjust that attitude.

He was a rather attractive young man, and he dressed dapperly, wearing suits of the latest style. He began attempting to sport a mustache, and for a time let his sideburns grow long.

Du Bois' superior manner, which bordered on arrogance, would eventually mellow somewhat after repeated confrontations with fellow students. Even some of the teachers, most of them white New Englanders, considered him overbearing and unkind. The young man had been taught that honesty was a virtue and that one must always tell the truth. Du Bois interpreted this to mean that

Most of the schools built for African-Americans in the late 19th century were one room buildings that employed one teacher for the entire school. Often she taught all twelve grades.

he must always *say* what he thought, holding nothing back, for he invariably voiced his opinions of everyone. Though this was generally done in a teasing, friendly manner, his wit was biting, even vicious.

Eventually he would learn that sometimes silence could be a virtue. After being the brunt of his biting wit once too often, O.C. Hunter, a powerfully built black student, grabbed Du Bois by the arm and squeezed, saying, "Don't you do that again!" Du Bois didn't, at least to Hunter.

His problems with another student, "Pop" Miller, were more serious. Miller was over twice Du Bois' age, and he had suffered hardships to try to get an education. He was the polar opposite of the brash young Yankee, being a southern black, devoutly religious, who worked hard and took everything seriously. He was an official of the Congregational Church at Fisk, which Du Bois had routinely joined. When Miller caught Du Bois dancing, he made a complaint against him in church to have him reprimanded. Du Bois saw no harm in dancing, and this slap became the second step in his move away from the Christian religion. He continued to write reports of his progress at Fisk to Reverend Painter because the church was paying his way through school, but he was not especially diligent in this chore.

However, Du Bois was beginning to understand and accept part of the objective of Painter, Van Lennep, and Hosmer in insisting on his studying in the South. Living among large numbers of African-Americans, almost all of them from the South, proved to be an important part of his education. The racial consciousness his mentors hoped he would acquire began to develop almost immediately, and within his first year at Fisk he had settled on the advancement of African-Americans as his life's purpose. Yet, because he was still so much farther advanced intellectually than he was emotionally, it was from the outset a cold, calculated decision, not one based upon personal experiences of hardship or suffering.

As a first step in this mission, he decided after his first year at Fisk to spend the summer teaching in a rural school. In addition to helping blacks who were less fortunate than he was, it would also provide much needed funds to supplement his scholarship for the second year.

When classes ended in the spring of 1886, he set out on the roads of East Tennessee in search of a community needing a teacher. Eventually, in an impoverished rural area near Alexandria, he came across a young woman named Josie who was two years older than he and was much excited by the prospects of having a school. She was thin, awkward, and unattractive, but she had boundless energy, and she directed Du Bois to all the people he would need to make arrangements with in order to open a school.

It was early July before he was able to begin his classes in a crude and poorly equipped log hut, and he was to be paid $28 a month this first year, raised to $30 the next summer. Those two summers were to be as educational for him as they were for his students. He was stunned by the living conditions of blacks in the rural South. Even years later he termed them "barbaric." It had never occurred to him that large families could live cramped into one-room hovels with dirt floors, wearing filthy rags and eating whatever could be obtained from day to day.

Yet he found these poor, simple people, who were eager to learn whatever he could teach them, to be endearing. In later years he would write of them with deep and sincere love. If he had never experienced the severe hardship of basic survival, he at least witnessed it among his students and their families.

He was provided no permanent living accommodations but roomed and boarded one night with one family, the next with another. The children were proud when the teacher came to stay, and their parents were honored. Always they tried to offer him the best they could of their meager provisions.

It was on one of these nights that Du Bois had his first sexual experience, and it was a disturbing one for him. Knowing nothing at all about sex at the time, he did not understand what was happening when the woman of the house, unhappy in her marriage, climbed into his bed and proceeded to have sex with him. Because of his puritanical New England upbringing, he was unable to deal with the experience emotionally or intellectually. Upon returning to Fisk, when he attempted to talk about it with other young men, they responded either by teasing him unmercifully or by disbelief at his ignorance and inexperience. It would be years before he would ever be able to resolve his conflicting attitudes about sex.

In most other ways, his second and third years at Fisk were maturing ones. Although he never compromised his competitiveness or his belief in honesty and directness in relationships, he did adapt himself socially by accepting the failings of others. He drifted further from organized religion, adamantly refusing to lead in public prayer, while becoming more

intrigued with philosophy and Negro spiri-
tuals, which he found devoutly meaningful.

Proud, but also insecure, he developed
characteristics at this time that would stay
with him throughout his life. As a protective
measure, he developed a reserve and a digni-
ty of manner that were beyond his years, rarely letting his deepest emotions show, whether
it was to evidence pain or sadness or to express
boisterous laughter. This manner was held
firmly when in the company of whites; it was
only with the most intimate of black friends
that he would let down his guard.

It was during his second year that he renewed his determination to attend Harvard to
study philosophy under William James, and he
began to apply for scholarship aid to go there
after graduation from Fisk.

He also became increasingly aware of the
political and social events of the time. Violence
against African-Americans, especially in the
South, was on the increase in the 1880s. With
the Reconstruction period over, power had
returned to southern whites, and efforts were
beginning to entirely disenfranchise blacks.
Lynchings were on the increase, and a concept
of formalized segregation of the races was in
its infancy. The cause of African-Americans
was regressing, not progressing, and young Du

Bois could see where things were heading. Fear of blacks by whites brought about violence, which in turn engendered fear of whites among blacks, creating a vicious, never-ending cycle.

Du Bois was frequently frightened by what he saw around him. Some of his fellow students carried guns or other weapons for protection. When the editor of the local paper was killed, Du Bois went down to the newspaper office to look at the bullet holes in the door of the building, trying to understand the senseless violence.

He did realize that the roots of prejudice and fear were sometimes subtle. In some ways it was an advantage to him having it as a new experience; in other ways it was not. While teaching in East Tennessee he perceived that the poor, uneducated rural blacks accepted unspoken rules of segregation without question. Yet, when he accidentally rubbed shoulders with a white woman on a crowded Nashville street and voiced a respectful apology, he could not comprehend the look of terrifying hatred the woman gave him.

It was a system that had to change, and it would be his life's mission to be instrumental in making those changes, though at this point he had no idea how he would go about it.

He did realize he had two special talents he could utilize, both of which he was developing during his last years at Fisk. He had natural oratorical abilities, for speaking publicly with passion and logic, and he could write the English language equally compellingly. During his senior year, he was made editor of the school paper, the *Fisk Herald,* in which he wrote strong and impressive editorials.

There was, in 1887, a controversy centering around the school. The Tennessee legislature was concerned that there were white students attending Fisk along with the blacks, and it threatened to withdraw state financial aid if the school did not become wholly segregated. The students and faculty were outraged at the demand; almost all of the white students were the children of the white professors at Fisk, and it seemed foolish to force them to go elsewhere to study. When the issue was pressed, it was virtually unanimous among students and administration to stand on principles; Fisk would give up state support rather than segregate.

In the spring of 1888, the end of his third year, du Bois graduated from Fisk, valedictorian in a class of five. All the students gave commencement orations, and Du Bois selected "Bismarck" as his topic. At the time he ad-

William James, a philosophy professor at Harvard, was Du Bois'
ideal. The young man was determined to go to Harvard to
study under him.

mired the leader who had united the bickering German states, considering him a model for African-Americans to emulate. Later, when he better understood the politics of Europe and the nature of imperialism, his views of the leader would change.

Before the school year had ended, everyone at Fisk was aware that Du Bois had been accepted to study at Harvard, and that he had been awarded a $250 scholarship, Price Greenleaf Aid, for his studies there. Even his professors were astonished by the news.

In order to earn money he would need for Harvard, Du Bois spent the summer of 1888 managing the Fisk Glee Club. The club was employed at a resort on Lake Minnetonka, Minnesota, where they doubled as both performers and waiters.

The experience at Lake Minnetonka was another shock to the young man's New England sensibilities. The drinking, the crude behavior, and the sexual promiscuity of the guests broadened his education considerably. As manager, Du Bois obtained bookings in Minnesota, Wisconsin, and Illinois and at the end of the summer each of the young men netted about $100.

Du Bois thought this bankroll would pay for his travel to Cambridge and get him off to a good start at Harvard, but he had some surprises ahead of him. The first occurred in Rochester, New York, when a young man woke him up hurriedly, asking him to exchange a ten-dollar bill for ten singles. In his sleepy state, Du Bois did not realize until the young man was off the train and gone that he had been handed only five dollars.

Arriving at Harvard with less than fifty dollars in cash left, he faced the second surprise. The Price Greenleaf Aid would not be available to him until later in the year, and he had to pay his $150 tuition immediately. It took considerable effort to get the scholarship fund to release part of the money in advance so that he could begin classes.

Another disappointment was that he had to register as a junior underclassman rather than a first year master's candidate because his education in high school and at Fisk was inadequate for Harvard's standards.

Du Bois' behavior at Harvard was curiously out of character and, while he has attempted to explain it differently in each of his three autobiographies, none of the explanations made complete sense, though his admission in *Dusk of Dawn* that it stemmed partially from an inferiority complex may be the truth. Now fully aware of the caste system in the United

In 1888, Du Bois graduated from Fisk University (where he was valedictorian) and set his sights on Harvard. He was awarded a $250 scholarship to Harvard. While at Fisk, he was editor of

the school paper, the Fisk Herald, *and wrote strong and impressive articles on the problems facing African-Americans.*

States, which existed in both North and South, he probably did not want to give others the opportunity to reject him. In any event, the young Fisk graduate went out of his way to avoid being noticed at Harvard.

Du Bois had returned to his native Massachusetts, yet he continued to abide by the segregated customs of the South. He did not even attempt to obtain lodging near the campus, but sought out a black boarding house. He rented a room from a woman on Flagg Street, where he stayed for his entire four years. He consciously avoided close contact with white students; only when white students sought him out did he associate with them. He made very few close friends, even among the school's black students, and devoted almost all of his time to his studies. Only once, when he was in need of the prize money, did he enter an oratory contest.

His goal was a degree in philosophy, and he finally achieved his long-held desire to study under the great William James. He benefitted from his studies, and from viewing his classmates from the sidelines, for he was growing to understand social conditions in the United States much better than if he had entered Harvard directly out of Great Barrington High School.

It was with the commencement exercises in June of 1890, when he was awarded his B.A. in philosophy from Harvard, that Du Bois first called attention to himself. Graduating *cum laude,* he was chosen as one of five students to speak at commencement, and he chose as his topic, "Jefferson Davis." His choice was clearly calculated to attract attention, and his approach to the subject was so fair that the *Nation* commented: "Du Bois handled his difficult and hazardous subject with absolute good taste, great moderation, and almost contemptuous fairness."

That spring, Du Bois also received a sum of money that would aid him in continuing in graduate school at Harvard. What was to him a small fortune at the time was $400 bequeathed to him in his grandfather Alexander Du Bois' will. Alexander had died in 1887, during W.E.B.'s final year at Fisk, but it had taken two years for the will to be probated.

In the fall of 1890, Du Bois enrolled in Harvard's graduate school. During registration he met a young African-American named Monroe Trotter, who was entering as a freshman undergraduate. They quickly became close friends, and their friendship and political association would last many years.

Chapter Four

A Voice
in Search
of a Platform

URING HIS LAST TWO years at Harvard, Du Bois continued to maintain a low profile with the white students, although he did at times associate with some of his professors outside of class, especially William James who frequently invited the young student to his home. Du Bois was working in history and political science toward his master's degree, but he was concentrating on the application of philosophy to the history of race relations, anticipating a field of study that would become sociology, a field in which he was to be one of the pioneers.

After graduating cum laude *from Harvard, Du Bois received an unexpected bequest from the estate of his grandfather, Alexander Du Bois, which aided him financially during graduate school.*

In more than one way Du Bois was venturing into uncharted territory, and he was cautious if not actually frightened. Because of his family background, the rules and strictures of society were very important to him. Years later he would reflect that, if he had been born white, he probably would have been rigidly conservative. However, being born black and reared with the puritanical values of New England created in him a paradox that would be with him throughout his life—a shy, reserved man who was bluntly outspoken, even belligerent.

He appears to have been fully aware that the more education he was obtaining, the less he fit into an identifiable social group. In 1891, he delivered a speech to the National Colored League of Boston on the topic, "Does Education Pay?" Of course his conclusion was an affirmative one, but it is clear he was questioning the matter, even though he later claimed that he had planned out the course of his life from the beginning.

Apparently, what he had planned was to be a voice for his people; what he could not have planned was the means by which he was to achieve this.

In December of 1891, he submitted the first draft of his master's thesis on "The Enforcement of the Slave Laws," which was well received, and in the spring of 1892 he received his master's degree. This thesis, which received wide attention, including his election to the American Historical Society, was to grow into his doctoral dissertation at Harvard, "The Suppression of the African Slave Trade to the United States of America." However, it was to be some time before he was to accomplish this, for he lacked the funds to continue his studies at Harvard.

Since 1890, he had been applying to the Slater Fund, which had been established in 1882 specifically to provide scholarships for the education of African-Americans. But former President Rutherford Hayes, who was administering the fund, scrupulously avoided allocating the money because he had as yet found no student worthy of the prize. Du Bois pressed the matter so strongly that he was finally awarded $750 by the fund, half grant and half loan, to study a year in Europe, with the possibility that he might obtain the same amount for a second year.

He traveled to New York to meet with Hayes at the Astor House and came out of the meeting so elated that he celebrated by buying himself a shirt costing an incredible three dollars.

In July of 1892 Du Bois set sail for Europe aboard a Dutch steamer, the *Amsterdam,* arriving on the first of August. He spent the first two months touring England, Holland, Germany, Austria, France, and Italy. From the moment he arrived there, his perspective of the world altered completely. He quickly realized that the United States was as insular in its viewpoint as Great Barrington had been. He said of the experience: "The unity of all life clutched me. I was not less fanatically a Negro, but 'Negro' meant a greater, broader sense of humanity and world fellowship. I felt myself standing, not against the world, but simply against American narrowness and color prejudice, with the greater, finer world at my back."

It was the beginning of a sense of "internationalism" that he would consider far more important than the prevailing attitude of "nationalism" that would provoke two world wars in the twentieth century.

In October of 1892, Du Bois enrolled at Friedrich Wilhelm University in Berlin, studying political science and economics. Although he had some difficulty understanding the German language of the lecturers and found it almost impossible to decipher their handwriting on the blackboard, he learned a great deal about the views and ideas that were shaping the modern world. He also broadened his love and understanding of music by attending the opera and musical concerts.

However, it was in his ability to relate to people that he gained the most by his experiences in Europe. He had accepted, and possibly even added to, the barriers between him and whites in his own country. It was very helpful to him to meet whites for whom his color was nothing more than an interesting physical distinction, because it taught him that what existed in the United States was an unnatural, socially imposed barrier. He later said of the experience: "I ceased to hate or suspect people simply because they belonged to one race or color."

He began to dress in the formal European style, and grew a full "handlebar" mustache with a Van Dyke beard, which he would continue to sport for the rest of his life.

Europe also broadened Du Bois' experiences with sex, though it did not resolve his moral or emotional conflicts regarding it. He tried an experience with a prostitute in Paris, but found that the idea offended his sense of decency. In Berlin, he lived openly with a "shop girl" for a time but was "ashamed." He also had a romance with an attractive young woman named Dora Marbach, watched over and approved by her parents, and she wanted to marry him and return to the United States with him, but he knew that would ultimately be a mistake.

As his year in Europe progressed, Du Bois began to be concerned that he had heard nothing from the Slater Fund about providing for the second year. There was some confusion about letters lost in trans-Atlantic transit, which caused him considerable anxiety, before another $750 was provided.

When that second year was over, there was no way for him to remain abroad; he had to return to his homeland and face the reality of the racial barriers there. However, he decided he could prolong his stay a bit longer by changing his means of transportation home; by booking steerage passage among emigrants he could have a few extra days of joy and enchantment.

After setting sail from Southampton aboard the *Chester,* an American ship, he had some second thoughts about his decision. The experience was much worse than he had expected, but he was able to chalk it up as a part of his education.

He was going home to face as much uncertainty as many of the emigrant passengers. He had no scholarship to continue his studies and, as yet, no job. He arrived with only enough money to pay his way to Great Barrington with two dollars to spare. Anxiously he wrote letters applying for teaching positions at all the black colleges he could—Howard, Hampton, Tuskegee, Fisk, and others—vowing that he would take the first offer he could get. The first to arrive was a telegram from Wilberforce University in Ohio, and he promptly accepted. Later, when he also received offers from Booker T. Washington at Tuskegee and from Lincoln Institute in Missouri, he would wonder if he hadn't been too hasty. Wilberforce had offered him $800 a year; Tuskegee's offer, which he had to turn down, was $1050 a year.

In August 1894 he traveled to Xenia, Ohio, to take on his new duties as chair of the classics department at Wilberforce, which was a very fine title but meant nothing more than that he was to teach Latin and Greek. Because of the limited resources of the college, he also covered German and English. Du Bois had hoped he would also be able to teach the newly developing subject of sociology, but the school's administration was not intellectually adventurous. Wilberforce was a rather small college, sponsored by the African Methodist Episcopal Church, with funds supplemented by the State of Ohio.

The idealistic twenty-six-year-old Du Bois was unprepared to deal with the realities of state and church politics that came with his teaching position. His blunt manner, combined with his disenchantment with organized religion, almost lost him the job in his first days on campus. Still becoming accustomed to the school, he dropped in on a student prayer meeting. As soon as he walked into the room, the student leading the meeting spotted him and announced, "Professor Du Bois will lead us in prayer." Du Bois promptly cut back, "No, he won't!" He was called before the board of bishops to explain his response, and he almost didn't talk his way out of being fired on the spot.

Although Du Bois was very unhappy at Wilberforce, the two years he spent there were important in his own education and development. He was an idealist and an intellectual; he had a phenomenal amount of book learning, especially for an African-American of his time, but he had virtually no experience in dealing with common, basic reality, also unusual for a black man in nineteenth-century America. He thought all he had to do to accomplish his ideals was to set his goals and follow a plan. In his long life he would never be able fully to accept a pragmatic approach to problems, but his first teaching experience taught him that life was not so easy as philosophy books implied.

Recognizing that Wilberforce was ruled by the whims of A.M.E. Bishop Benjamin Arnett, Du Bois bent slightly, just enough to stay within the rules, but he recognized from the outset that he would not last long there. He maintained his full course load and fulfilled his other duties, which included student discipline, during the days; he spent his evenings completing the final draft of his doctoral dissertation for Harvard.

When submitted, the dissertation was accepted, and in the spring of 1895 he received his PhD from Harvard. A year later his dissertation, *The Suppression of the African Slave-Trade to the United States of America, 1638-1870,* was published as a book. Du Bois was beginning to make a name for himself that was gradually spreading outward from the educational community.

However, this would make little difference when a confrontation finally came between him and Bishop Arnett. Du Bois knew he was sealing his fate when he led students and faculty in opposition to the Bishop's attempt to appoint his unqualified ne'er-do-well son,

Upon finishing graduate school, Du Bois accepted the first job offer, for $800 per year, from Wilberforce University in Ohio. Soon after accepting, he received another offer from Booker T.

Washington at Tuskegee Institute (shown here) to teach there for more money, an offer he regrettably had to refuse since he was already committed.

Ben Arnett, as professor of American literature. Under pressure Arnett backed down, but he did everything possible to make Du Bois uncomfortable thereafter.

One of Du Bois' more unpleasant experiences at Wilberforce was probably not calculated by Bishop Arnett. In February of 1896, classes were suspended while the college held a revival meeting downstairs in the building where Du Bois lived. He did not attend the meetings, but shut himself into his room. However, he could not avoid hearing what he described as the "wild screams, cries, groans and shrieks" emanating from the chapel day after day.

A part of the plan that Du Bois had set out for himself was to be married by the time he was thirty. When he met Nina Gomer, a young student from Iowa, he decided that she suited his ideals for a wife. She was both beautiful and intelligent, and as an added attraction, Nina's German mother had trained her in the old country's efficient methods of housekeeping, which Du Bois had admired during his time abroad. He would later admit that this dispassionate decision had been a mistake, because at the time he was still sexually inexperienced and romantically naive. However, even though they proved to be ill-suited to each

Booker T. Washington, head of the Tuskegee Institute in Alabama, became the forerunner of black spokespersons when he made a speech which was referred to as "the Atlanta Compromise."

other, the couple would make the marriage work for almost forty years.

Because of the school's casual attitude about paying its teachers, the wedding almost did not take place. On the eve of the day set for the ceremony, Du Bois still had not received his overdue paycheck. He tracked down the Wilberforce treasurer, who was preparing to board a train for a conference, and pressured the man into paying him so he could attend his wedding. On May 12, 1896, he rushed to Cedar Rapids, Iowa, met Nina's father, the chef of the main hotel in the town, and married Nina. Then the couple hurried back to Xenia, Ohio, so that Du Bois could teach classes the next day.

Aware that his position at Wilberforce could not last long, Du Bois had been sending out letters of application to other educational institutions. Shortly after his marriage he received an offer from the University of Pennsylvania. It had several drawbacks. It was an appointment for only one year, and his position would be assistant instructor in sociology. Even though Du Bois had received his doctorate from Harvard at this point, the University of Pennsylvania would not make him a full instructor because he was black. And the salary would be only $900 for the year.

Despite the drawbacks, there were attractions for Du Bois, the main one being that it was in the new field of sociology, his primary interest. Another was that he would not really be teaching but conducting a sociological study of the basis for political corruption in Philadelphia's Seventh Ward, which was a black slum. He was not unaware that the government-funded program was based upon the hope that the study would prove all of Philadelphia's problems could be blamed on the vice-ridden black neighborhood. He considered it a great opportunity to do the kind of work he wanted to do.

For lodging, the newlyweds took one room over a cafeteria in the worst section of the Seventh Ward. It must have been a frightening experience for Nina, for Du Bois has described their year there as being "in the midst of an atmosphere of dirt, drunkenness, poverty, and crime. Murder sat on our doorsteps, police were our government, and philanthropy dropped in with periodic advice." He was so enthralled with his work that he probably was unaware of how his new wife was dealing with the situation.

Du Bois was aware that he was paving new ground in the field of sociology. He was creating methods and a framework that would be utilized by other similar studies in the future. The work would last six months longer than intended, and the results would be far more than what the City of Philadelphia had wanted. When they would finally be published in 1898 in book form as *The Philadelphia Negro,* it would be a landmark in the field of sociology. However, at the time, only scholars were willing to read through the lengthy volume to appreciate it.

While he was in Philadelphia, Du Bois received an offer from Horace Bumstead, President of Atlanta University, to set up the school's "Negro Problem" program, which would involve extensive sociological studies over a ten-year period. Du Bois accepted eagerly, setting up the first subject immediately for 1896, *Mortality among Negroes in Cities,* even though he could not move to Atlanta until the fall of 1897, when he had completed compiling the data for the Philadelphia study.

At Atlanta, Du Bois would be professor of history and economics, teaching classes as well as conducting research and producing studies of the problems of blacks in America. He and Nina moved there with their newborn son, Burghardt Gomer Du Bois, with promises of a long and happy future. Nina, who was less interested in scholarly matters than she was in having a family and living comfortably, was glad to be leaving the Philadelphia slums and settling down in one place for a full ten years.

Certainly, in the beginning, Du Bois was happy. He found his young black students at Atlanta eager and excited to learn and to forge new ground. When a possible conflict arose about the necessity of classroom prayer, Du Bois compromised and agreed to use the *Book of Common Prayer,* though he did not always live up to his promise.

Of course there were some frustrations, such as when he pressed the Federal Bureau of Labor Statistics to try to persuade them to build on the Philadelphia study by pursuing other sociological studies, only to be ignored. However, for the most part he was satisfied that he was finally acquiring a platform for his ideas and goals. By the time he was thirty, he had published two books and three of the scheduled ten *Atlanta University Studies— Mortality among Negroes in Cities, Social and Physical Conditions of Negroes in Cities,* and *Some Efforts of Negroes for Social Betterment.*

Increasingly, Du Bois was being asked to speak at important conferences, such as the American Academy of Political and Social Sciences in 1897 and the Negro Businessmen of Chicago in 1898. He was also frequently asked to contribute articles to national journals and magazines.

Even his married life seemed to be improving since the birth of Burghardt, who was now almost two years old. But in 1899, tragedy struck. The child became seriously ill, a victim of a sewage problem in Atlanta's water system, and died. In his grief, Du Bois was able to throw himself even more into his work, but Nina had no such escape. She fell into a despondency from which she would never fully recover. Even though another child, a daughter named Yolande, was born the following year, the bright spark of hope for happiness in life was gone from her. She continued to endure as the dutiful wife for years, but strived for nothing more. Her own emotional state was to grow worse in 1906 when she was faced with the horror of the Atlanta race riots.

Whether it was the loss of the child or the change in Nina, or a combination of both, Du Bois became even more distant and restrained with students and associates, never letting his emotions show publicly.

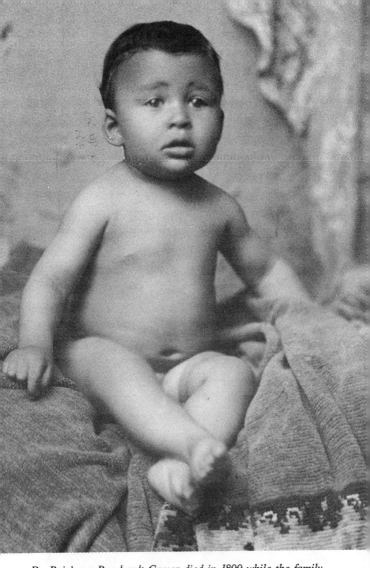

Du Bois' son Burghardt Gomer died in 1899 while the family lived in Atlanta. The child's sickness could be directly attributed to the sewage problem in Atlanta's water system.

Chapter Five

Competing for Leadership

H IGHLY COMPETITIVE EVEN AS a child, Du Bois probably could not have prevented himself from competing with established black leaders once he began to acquire a wide audience, even if he had wanted to. Since 1895, the acknowledged spokesman for African-Americans had been Booker T. Washington. In September of that year, Washington had made a speech that became known as "the Atlanta Compromise" at the Atlanta Cotton & International Exposition, which had stirred both blacks and whites with a new concept of "separate but equal." At the

Du Bois in Paris in 1900. Du Bois won a gold medal in the 1900 Paris Exibition on African-American life. While in Europe, he attended the first Pan-African Congress.

time, young W.E.B. Du Bois had been as admiring as everyone else, but gradually that would change.

Washington and Du Bois had corresponded with each other long before they ever met face to face, beginning in 1894 when Du Bois had applied to teach at Tuskegee only to accept the position at Wilberforce before hearing from Washington.

In 1899, they finally met in Boston, when they were invited to share a podium with poet Paul Laurence Dunbar at the Hollis Street Theater. Even though opposite in background and temperament, the two men liked each other. They already had differing viewpoints about solutions to the problems of African-Americans, but they considered their differences less important than the overall goal of advancement.

For almost five years they were able to work together without serious problems, beginning with a plan for cooperation between Atlanta University and Hampton Institute in 1899. In 1900, when Washington was asked for his recommendation of a person to be superintendent of the black schools in Washington, D.C., his first choice was Du Bois, but Du Bois turned down the offer because of other commitments. They also cooperated in efforts to change the policy of railroads in supplying separate and unequal facilities for blacks, the notorious "Jim Crow cars," which were little more than poorly fitted baggage or freight cars. In doing this they followed Washington's approach of quiet but firm private pressure.

In 1900, Du Bois was asked to set up an exhibit on African-American life for the Paris Exposition, which gave him an opportunity to travel to Europe again. Although he was provided with only a small room for his exhibit space, the display he assembled won a gold medal and attracted much attention. While he was abroad, he went to London to attend the first Pan-African Congress. Although little would come of the efforts at this time, this meeting was the beginning of attempts to unify blacks from all over the world with an objective of gaining independence for African nations. Du Bois was elected chairman of the congress, and his experiences here would be a strong influence in his developing a sense of internationalism, unifying people of like minds all over the world, whatever their nationality.

Although Booker T. Washington remained the preeminent spokesman for African-Americans, Du Bois was developing an increasingly growing number of supporters, especially black intellectuals, who were concerned that the older leader had given away too much in the Atlanta Compromise. In all his writings and comments on the matter, Du Bois never made entirely clear how he changed from supporter of Washington to vocal opponent. It would appear that he had mixed feelings from the beginning.

From the time he was a student at Fisk, Du Bois had believed that separation of blacks and whites, at least in the United States, was necessary. He went so far as to maintain a distance between sympathetic northern whites and himself, believing that ultimately their goals could not coincide. Washington believed that blacks and whites could go their separate ways but cooperate on matters of mutual interest.

In the decades just before and after the turn of the century, conditions for blacks all over the country were growing increasingly worse. Segregated housing laws were being enacted, laws limiting the right to vote, and with a rash of lynchings and riots even the right to the protection of the law was being infringed. To many young, educated African-Americans, Washington's moderate approach appeared only to encourage this trend, and they began to advocate stronger means of resistance.

One of the most radical and outspoken opponents of Booker T. Washington now coming to prominence was Du Bois' old friend from Harvard, Monroe Trotter, who in 1901 began publication of the *Boston Guardian,* a journal promoting black political action. Du Bois insisted he did not "wholly agree" with Trotter's approach, and he walked the fence between the two strongly opposing sides until events catapulted him into Trotter's camp.

At least to some extent Du Bois may have consciously brought about some of these events. Certainly he must have known what Washington's reaction would be when he wrote the essay "Of Mr. Booker T. Washington and Others" for inclusion in *The Souls of Black Folk,* which was written in 1902 but published in 1903. Probably the most successful of Du Bois' books, this collection of essays came at the request of a publisher, and he did not consider it to be a major work at the time. However, it was less academic than most of his writings and therefore more popular.

Blunt and honest as always, Du Bois unleashed a scathing attack on Washington's conciliatory approach, which stunned the leader, who had thought Du Bois his friend. Washington did not fight back but continued his association with Du Bois, though

The president of Atlanta University asked Du Bois to head the school's "Negro Problem" program, instituted to put down on paper just exactly the nature of the problems so that decisive

answers could be attained. While in Atlanta, Du Bois also taught history and economics as well as conducting research for this program.

cautiously. While others were already talking about a rift between the two men, they jointly launched a protest against the Rhodes Trust for excluding black candidates from its scholarship program, and they continued their efforts to rid the railroads of Jim Crow cars.

On July 30, 1903, Booker T. Washington was scheduled to address the National Negro Business League at the Columbus Avenue A.M.E. Zion Church in Boston. A group of black radicals, led by Monroe Trotter and his partner in the *Boston Guardian*, George Forbes, was determined to break up the meeting and prevent Washington from being heard. They sprinkled pepper on the podium beforehand and heckled the three speakers who preceded Washington. When Washington rose to address the assemblage, a fist-fight broke out, which rapidly grew into a riot. One man was stabbed, and Monroe Trotter took over the podium to yell out accusations at Washington. The police were called to calm things, but when they arrived they were surrounded by screaming women who attempted to prevent them from restoring order until the men in blue threatened to use their clubs.

Five of the ringleaders were arrested— Monroe Trotter, his sister Maude Trotter (who was accused of stabbing a policeman with her hatpin), Bernard Charles (who had been stabbed), and a butler named Granville Martin. Maude Trotter was released, but the organizers of the event pressed charges against the other three.

Upon hearing the news, possibly inaccurately, Du Bois wrote an angry attack upon Washington for "strangling honest criticism." The rift between Du Bois and Washington was widening rapidly.

A conference was called in New York, sponsored by Andrew Carnegie, for January of 1904, in the hopes of resolving problems and unifying African-American leadership. Washington and Du Bois remained cordial but cool when they shared the podium at Carnegie Hall. Both men were appointed to the Committee of Twelve, which was to be a steering committee to maintain the unity. The effort would prove to be a dismal failure.

The year 1905 was a turning point; it had been forty years since the end of the Civil War, and an entire generation, both black and white, had grown to full maturity with no direct memories of that conflict. Just as the younger whites sought to turn back the clock, so were the younger blacks determined to move forward. If the older generation would not let go of leadership, the new would force the issue and wrest it from their hands.

Afterwards, Du Bois consistently denied that he ever sought to be a spokesman or a leader for African-Americans, yet his character and his actions suggest otherwise. In January of 1905, he again attacked Washington in print. In an article, "Debit and Credit," published in *The Voice of the Negro* that month, he described what he called "The Tuskegee Machine," which he claimed was led by Booker T. Washington and unnamed white political and business leaders with the objective of controlling black leadership in America. The basis for the accusation was that Washington had served as advisor to presidents William McKinley and Theodore Roosevelt, recommending blacks qualified for appointments, and had curried the favor of businessmen like Andrew Carnegie to obtain funds for Tuskegee.

Du Bois was widely criticized for not substantiating his accusation, but the existence of the Tuskegee Machine came to be accepted as fact, and there was some organized resistance to Du Bois and Trotter from Tuskegee in the years that followed.

Du Bois was beginning to develop a philosophical basis for his differences with Washington, a concept he called "The Talented

Andrew Carnegie, businessman and philanthropist, called together a meeting in 1904 with the hopes of unifying African-American leadership. Both Du Bois and Washington appeared.

Tenth." He had long been critical of the kind of industrial training espoused by Washington and exemplified by the programs at Tuskegee and Hampton. He felt it was a waste to educate large numbers of African-Americans to do no more than work as skilled laborers; he believed it would ultimately be more beneficial to the race to concentrate efforts on giving higher education to the top ten percent, the most intelligent, who would become professional men and leaders, who would then make the needed changes in society. It was an interesting theory, though rather elitist, and he proposed no means of selecting the top ten percent for education.

There was no longer any possibility of cooperation between the young intellectuals and the established leadership of Booker T. Washington. Du Bois issued a call to those who were in sympathy with him to meet in Buffalo, New York, on July 9, 1905, with the objective of forming a new organization. This meeting was to take place in secret, and neither Booker T. Washington nor any of his supporters would be welcome. Twenty-nine representatives from fourteen states showed up, all of them what Du Bois considered the "very best class of Negro Americans," young educated professionals—talented, though hardly a tenth of the black population. When the group ran into problems of discrimination at the hotel they had reserved, they picked up and moved across the border to the Canadian side of the Niagara Falls at Ft. Erie.

Thus the organization came to be named the "Niagara Movement," and it was incorporated in Washington, D.C., on January 31, 1906. Du Bois and Trotter were the acknowledged leaders from the outset, and they wrote most of the new organization's "Declaration of Principles," which were soundly based and well formulated, though southern whites considered them "radical." They asked for the rights guaranteed by the Fourteenth and Fifteenth Amendments, which were rapidly being taken away by state laws—full manhood suffrage, repeal of peonage laws in the South (which were returning many to a condition not unlike slavery), right to free public education through the high-school level, the right to free speech and free press, and equal treatment in the judicial system, both in jury selection and in punishment of the guilty.

No reasonable person could disagree with these demands; they were just and necessary. There were, however, a few items included that could not be universally agreed upon and probably could not have been legislated, at least at the time. Yet it is possible that Du Bois and Trotter set forth the principles with the realization that simple justice could be achieved by asking for full justice, that compromise could best be achieved by not acknowledging a willingness to compromise at the outset. They asked for free college education for a talented tenth of African-Americans; they asked that labor unions open their membership to blacks; they asked that employers be prevented from hiring blacks only on a temporary basis as needed; and they asked for the opportunity to live in clean and healthy surroundings.

The approach they set forth to accomplish these ends was one that many at the time disagreed with. They proposed federal legislation to defeat the new unjust state laws; they called for "persistent manly agitation"; and they attacked Booker T. Washington's leadership approach as one of "cowardice and apology."

Du Bois was elected executive director of the Niagara Movement, and he remained at the helm during its short history, though Monroe Trotter and Clement Morgan participated at the highest level of leadership. When news of their organization reached the press, they and it were heavily criticized for meeting secretly as well as for the means they were proposing to achieve justice. For that reason they decided to hold their second annual meeting in public at Harper's Ferry, Virginia, yet they would never give in to opening their membership to all African-Americans who wished to join.

Largely because it was an elitist group, the Niagara Movement ultimately had to fail, but its brief life did have an important effect on African-American history, for it signaled the end of Booker T. Washington's approach of black and white compromise. Washington would find that he had to compromise not just with southern whites but with radical blacks as well.

For a time the feud between Du Bois and Washington would fragment the little power that African-Americans possessed, and race relations in the United States would worsen as a result. However, eventually the mantle of leadership would pass on to Du Bois, and the struggle for justice would be able to move forward again. Yet the mantle would never rest comfortably or naturally on Du Bois' shoulders. Blunt and outspoken, he would forever find himself at the center of controversy.

Chapter Six

A Loud,
Clear
Voice

THE CONCEPTS AND IDEAS behind the Niagara Movement were almost entirely those of W.E.B. Du Bois. At times other members attempted to disagree with him, but he had such a powerful personality and such a strong and passionate manner that he would invariably override the opinions of others, probably without realizing he was doing it. On an intellectual level, he believed very strongly in freedom of speech and criticism, yet he did not respond well when criticism was directed against him because he believed firmly that he was right, a normal human failing

---

Among the African-Americans who disagreed vehemently with Booker T. Washington's views of turn of the century racial problems in America was William Monroe Trotter.

though one a public figure has to overcome.

In the first two decades of the twentieth century, Du Bois was becoming a public figure. Each year, the Atlanta Studies Program produced another publication under his supervision, completing the initial ten—*The Negro in Business* (1899), *The College-Bred Negro* (1900), *The Negro Common School* (1901), *The Negro Artisan* (1902), *The Negro Church* (1903), *Notes on Negro Crime* (1904), and *A Select Bibliography on the American Negro* (1905). The Program had been so successful, Atlanta extended it for an additional ten years. As it would turn out, Du Bois would supervise only eight of those studies.

In 1906, when he was invited to speak at a Hampton Institute conference, Du Bois attracted considerable attention by using the platform to attack the very concept of Hampton, its industrial education program. As a result, he would not be invited back to the prestigious black school for twenty-five years.

That year the Niagara Movement held its open conference at Harper's Ferry, Virginia, probably the most successful and least controversial of its annual meetings, but still attracting widespread criticism. Du Bois invoked the name of John Brown to unify the group, and there was one very moving experience when the group of delegates rose at dawn and walked barefoot to the scene of John Brown's raid. Yet the criticism, even from prominent Niagara members, persisted. Most significant was the exclusivity of the membership itself. These critics realized that Niagara could not really be successful without mass support, and that could not exist while membership was denied to common laborers, the class that represented the majority of the African-American population.

Another important basis for criticism was the means proposed for achieving the Niagara's goals. The fact that Du Bois and Trotter proposed "agitation" as a legitimate way to achieve equality bothered some people. It was largely because of this criticism that the president of Storer College, which had hosted the 1906 meeting, withdrew his invitation for Niagara to meet there a second time.

Relations between blacks and whites in the United States reached a crisis point in 1906 with race riots in Brownsville, Texas, and Atlanta, Georgia. The new restrictive laws taking rights away angered blacks, and the new intellectual class of blacks talking about agitation created fear among whites. Both sides were growing increasingly belligerent toward each other.

The Niagara Movement held its annual meeting for 1907 in Springfield, Massachusetts, and it was marked by a feud between Monroe Trotter and Clement Morgan, which had begun as a local problem in Boston but had grown until it threatened to destroy the organization. Morgan had been with Du Bois' at Harvard, and in fact had been selected class orator. When Du Bois supported Morgan over Trotter in the dispute, and Niagara's executive committee supported Trotter, Du Bois threatened to resign. The executive committee gave in, but the organization's two principal leaders no longer trusted each other, and grew increasingly farther apart.

In 1906, Du Bois had begun publishing a small weekly newspaper called *The Moon,* which was printed in Memphis but which sought a national distribution among educated blacks. It offered a more radical viewpoint than the *Outlook,* the nation's leading weekly newspaper, which had been critical of him and of the Niagara Movement. Du Bois struggled with *The Moon* for a year and finally gave it up in favor of a new publication. In January of 1907, in partnership with F.H.M. Murray and L.M. Hershaw, he founded *The Horizon,* which he termed a "miniature monthly." This publication fared somewhat better because

Hershaw owned a printing company and because the three partners subsidized it. Each was responsible for writing individual issues, with their bylines, and Du Bois used it as a voice for the Niagara Movement. *The Horizon* would continue publication until July of 1910, when *The Crisis,* the official publication of the NAACP, would be founded and Du Bois selected to edit it.

These publications enabled Du Bois to make his voice heard on a wide variety of issues, whether it was as small as an attack on Booker T. Washington or as large an issue as Belgian imperialism in the Congo. He also contributed articles to many of the nation's leading magazines, such as *Colliers, The Nation, World's Work, The Atlantic Monthly,* and *Dial.*

Since Emancipation, African-Americans had voted Republican consistently, and in every presidential election year except 1884 and 1892, when Grover Cleveland was elected, Republicans had carried the field. Yet gradually blacks had been stripped of their rights. The Republican Party claimed it had been responsible for ending slavery, and therefore it deserved the loyalty of blacks. The Democratic Party had been dominated by white southerners before the war, and therefore it should always carry the burden of being the

In every presidental election, with the exception of 1884 and 1892, blacks were strong supporters of the Republicans. This started to change in the early 1900s as the very people elected

to office began to strip the African-American of their basic
rights. The republican government justified the the lynching of
blacks as a lesser crime than rape.

party of slavery.

Du Bois believed that the vote of African-Americans should not be taken for granted. The behavior of President Theodore Roosevelt and his Secretary of War, William Howard Taft, who was the Republican candidate for president in 1908, in dealing with the Brownsville Riot and the Atlanta Riot in 1906 had been as reprehensible as any Democrat could have been, for they justified the lynching of blacks as a lesser crime than the rape of white women by blacks, which had occurred in a few isolated but sensational cases. The implication was that the two crimes were invariably linked, which was untrue.

For years, Republican presidents had relied on Booker T. Washington as their advisor on African-American matters, and Du Bois considered that his conciliatory approach had been largely at fault for the rapid disintegration of black rights.

In February of 1908, Du Bois called on African-Americans to boycott the election that year, to give both political parties the message that the black vote should not be taken for granted. He was probably aware that the absence of blacks from the polls would give an advantage to the Democratic Party candidates, and he obviously had questions about the kind of message such a passive demonstration would convey. The right to vote was important, and blacks were rapidly losing that right in the South. That very year, one more southern state restricted black rights when Georgia amended its constitution to disenfranchise them.

In April, Du Bois changed his plea, now calling on African-Americans to support the Democratic Party candidate, William Jennings Bryan. Though Bryan was an acknowledged racist, he was the underdog in the campaign against William Howard Taft, and Du Bois believed blacks could swing the election, giving both parties an important message: blacks in the North could still vote, and their voices should be heard.

However, black voters did not hear Du Bois; when it was time to go to the polls, they voted as always for the Republican candidates, and William Howard Taft was elected president. Taft, like Roosevelt and McKinley, turned to Booker T. Washington for advice.

Du Bois experienced another disappointing rejection that year, though it was one of lesser importance. In an attempt to convey that black Americans were not only black but also American, he had applied for membership in the Sons of the American Revolution, for which he certainly qualified. The Massachusetts board accepted him, but when his application was received by the national board it was turned down.

The event of 1908 that proved to be the turning point in African-American civil rights was a race riot that took place in Springfield, Illinois, the hometown of Abraham Lincoln. It sent a shock wave throughout the entire country when a mob of whites there killed six blacks and drove about two-thousand more from the city. If such senseless violence could occur in Lincoln's home, it could occur in any town in the United States. It had to stop.

Northern white liberals who had long supported the advancement of African-Americans had grown increasingly dismayed by the fragmentation of black leadership, as well as by the rapid erosion of black rights and power in the United States. Unless some means could be found to unify the supporters of the various leaders—Washington, Du Bois, and Trotter being the principal ones—African-Americans would be kept in servitude forever. Most prominent among these white leaders were Oswald Garrison Villard, Mary White Ovington, and Charles E. Russell. Villard was a grandson of abolitionist William Lloyd Garrison and heir to a railroad fortune. He led the way in calling for a unifying meeting to be held in New York on the hundredth anniversary of Abraham Lincoln's birth, February 12, 1909. Joining in on the call were such important figures as Jane Addams, John Dewey, William Dean Howells, Lincoln Steffens, and J.G. Phelps-Stokes. In approaching Du Bois, Villard had to dismiss his personal feelings at what he considered a betrayal by Du Bois, who had just written and published a biography of John Brown, knowing that Villard had been working on one for years.

Both Booker T. Washington and Monroe Trotter refused to attend the conference. Du Bois was one of only six blacks who answered the call, which resulted in the formation of the National Association for the Advancement of Colored People, and one of these, Ida B. Wells-Barnett, chairman of the Anti-Lynching League, attended but refused to join the new organization. At its inception, the NAACP was primarily a white organization and thus had little likelihood of succeeding. By May of 1910, when the group met for the election of officers, its membership included only ten blacks, and only one—W.E.B. Du Bois—was on the slate of officers.

Despite his distrust of white liberals, Du Bois was willing to give the NAACP a chance.

It may have been at least partially due to
realizations that his efforts in 1908 had been
ineffective and that it was time to try a different approach. Certainly he was aware that
his situation at Atlanta University had become
precarious. Edmund Ware, who had succeeded Horace Bumstead as president of the
school, was personally supportive of Du Bois
and what he was trying to achieve, but financial supporters of the institution objected to
Du Bois' outspokenness, his constant agitation, and his political activities. And Du Bois
had been received coolly when he approached
backers to fund creation of an "Encyclopedia
Africana."

By the spring of 1910, Atlanta University's
financial situation had become so serious that
Ware had no choice but to accept the board's
request to relieve Du Bois of his position, ap-
pointing Augustus Dill to replace him in car-
rying on the work of the Atlanta Studies Program. Du Bois would be permitted to do the
editing on the publications through 1913.

When word reached New York of what had
happened, the NAACP offered Du Bois a
salaried position as their first director of
publicity and research. In July he moved to
New York and promptly began work on
creating an official journal for the new

organization, *The Crisis,* which he would edit. Some members of the board objected to the magazine because it gave Du Bois a forum for his opinions that the rest of them would not have, but it would be *The Crisis* that would be largely responsible for the early success of the NAACP, for it would create a link between the national office in New York and the many small local offices around the country.

Except for Trotter and Wells-Barnett, the Niagara Movement became incorporated into the new organization, which did not have elitist requirements for membership. In fact, it sought the broadest spectrum possible—both white and black—to join in seeking progress for African-Americans through education, legal action, and organization.

From the outset there were problems between Du Bois and Villard, who was chairman of the board as well as acknowledged founder of the organization. Their disagreements were complicated by the fact that Du Bois was not only a hired employee but also a member of the board. Du Bois sought to create a faction that would support him in disputes with Villard, and he found allies in Joel Spingarn, a Columbia University professor, whom everyone in the organization appeared to like, and Mary White Ovington.

In December of 1918, Du Bois was sent to France to attend the Versailles Peace Conference, where he hoped to be heard on the issues of African-Americans not only in the United States,

but in the world at large. He was disappointed, however, for he found that the major powers of the world, and especially England, were turning a deaf ear to his pleas.

Du Bois shared the NAACP's first offices at 20 Vesey Street in New York with another hired employee, the Executive Secretary, who had the job of fund-raising initially, and with whatever board members came in to volunteer time. He brought out the first issue of *The Crisis* in November 1910, and he would continue to be its voice until 1934. These years, from his forty-second to his sixty-sixth, would be among the most exciting for W.E.B. Du Bois, a time of personal and intellectual growth as well as of power and influence among African-Americans.

In 1911, the year of the NAACP's legal incorporation, he published his first novel, *The Quest for the Silver Fleece,* and he was invited to be the principal speaker at the International Congress of Races in London. That year, taking up residence in New York City, he also became so interested in the concepts of socialism that he briefly joined the Socialist Party. Although he was not always receptive to the opinions of others, he would throughout his life be entranced by the new ideas and philosophical beliefs of others.

For an even briefer period in 1912, Du Bois became interested in the Progressive Party and the "Bull Moose" candidacy of former President Theodore Roosevelt. In concept, both the NAACP and the Progressive Party were a part of the new "progressive" movement in the United States—a movement that sought to remove impediments to individual freedom and development. It is not known what made Du Bois think Roosevelt had changed since his mishandling of the Brownsville Riot in 1906, but in hopes of fair treatment from the new party, Du Bois drafted a civil rights plank for the Progressive platform and sent it to the Chicago convention by Joel Spingarn. The platform was not used, and the former president warned Spingarn to be wary of Du Bois, whom he considered "dangerous."

Rebuffed, Du Bois turned to support the Democratic Party candidate, Woodrow Wilson, who also claimed to be progressive, despite some openly expressed anti-black sentiments. Through an intermediary, Du Bois obtained a signed message from Wilson, stating: "I want to assure them that, should I become President of the United States, they may count upon me for absolute fair dealing, for everything by which I could assist in advancing the interests of their race in the United States."

This was the most Du Bois could expect from any politician of the period. He promptly resigned from the Socialist Party and devoted *The Crisis* to persuading blacks to vote for Wilson. A great many—an estimated one-hundred-thousand—heeded his call, for the first time abandoning the Republican Party. It was an important step for African-Americans, many of them realizing that they no longer owed unquestioned allegiance to any party and that their vote was something they could barter to gain and hold their rights.

Heady from what he considered a personal victory, Du Bois attempted to throw his weight around even more than he had before. For some members of the NAACP board, particularly for chairman Oswald Garrison Villard, the situation was growing intolerable. Villard believed *The Crisis* should, from time to time, include opinions of other members of the organization rather than always maintain only Du Bois' ideas. The objective of the NAACP was for its members to cooperate, not to compete with each other.

As early as 1911, in response to a sensational lynching case at Coatesville, Pennsylvania, Du Bois had begun to call upon blacks to arm themselves against white violence, and in 1912 he had condemned Secretary of the Navy Josephus Daniels for seizing Haiti to preserve order there and

Oswald Garrison Villard, chairman on the NAACP, was a vocal critic of Du Bois' writings in The Crisis, *stating that Du Bois should give equal voice to other members of the organization.*

crusaded against "U.S. imperialism." And when Woodrow Wilson did not live up to Du Bois' expectations during his first months in office, he began to attack him. He also continued to espouse his own elitist views, writing encouragements in *The Crisis* to "the thousand best people" to join the NAACP, and he was heavily criticized for printing a two-page photograph of himself among a group of blacks in Baltimore dressed in evening clothes.

Du Bois took Villard's criticism as an attempt to censor him and launched an attack on Villard that included disparaging remarks about his wife because she did not invite blacks to dine in her home. And he did not keep his attacks within the confines of the NAACP, but spoke against his associates from public platforms. Joel Spingarn, Du Bois' best friend on the board, attempted to mediate the dispute, which began to become serious in March of 1913. Throughout the year, Villard continued to be conciliatory but firm; Du Bois remained obstinate and unbending—he and he alone controlled what would appear in *The Crisis*, and he would not be dictated to by a man who was not only white but whom he considered to be a racist.

Finally, in January of 1914, to avoid the NAACP collapsing from the dispute, Villard resigned from chairmanship of the board, and Spingarn was elected to replace him. Very quickly, Du Bois turned his vicious tongue on the man who had been his best friend on the board. Spingarn bore it for awhile, but before the year was out, he wrote Du Bois a stinging letter, in which he informed him that the only reason Du Bois won arguments was the reason that parents give in to spoiled children—to avoid a scene—and that if Du Bois persisted in bickering with everyone on the board he would have to leave. Spingarn also reminded Du Bois that the NAACP paid for the publication of *The Crisis* and that it paid his salary.

Du Bois gave in only so far as to agree that he was sometimes difficult to get along with, then proceeded to do things his own way.

In 1915, with the death of Booker T. Washington, Du Bois would have what he had long sought—the unchallenged position as the leading spokesman for African-Americans. In writing of Washington's death in *The Crisis,* Du Bois was gracious in calling him the most important southerner since the Civil War and in ranking him with Frederick Douglass as a black leader, but he could not resist repeating his belief that setbacks in civil rights during the last twenty years had been Washington's fault.

Chapter Seven

A World Stage

THE OUTBREAK OF World War I in Europe provided W.E.B. Du Bois with an opportunity to have his broader views of racial problems heard. Although most social commentators considered the Balkan states to be at the heart of the European problems, Du Bois believed the conflict actually to be over which of the imperialistic powers would control Africa. Agreeing with Woodrow Wilson to some extent, he hoped the ultimate result of American involvement in the war would be to guarantee self-determination to the smaller, emerging nations; this, he felt, would prevent

Charles Evans Hughs, who ran as the republican candidate for president, was asked how he stood on civil rights but as he gave no reply, Du Bois gave his support to the Socialist Party.

an otherwise inevitable worldwide conflict between the lighter and darker races.

After the death of Booker T. Washington, there were attempts to unite African-American leadership to combat the widening breach between whites and blacks. To avoid criticism of adding to the divisiveness, the NAACP in 1916 postponed its annual conference, scheduled for Lincoln's birthday, to avoid competing with a special tribute to Washington. Joel Spingarn personally sponsored the most successful of these attempts at unification by inviting the leaders of all the important factions to his farm at Amenia, New York in August of that year.

Two-hundred invitations were sent out, and sixty black and white leaders, representing all factions, attended, from Emmett Scott, who had inherited the role of Booker T. Washington, to Monroe Trotter. The meeting was a harmonious one, in which all were willing to compromise and to attempt to work together. It was the most unified blacks had been since Reconstruction. Even Du Bois believed it marked the beginning of a new era in African-American history, though not in civil rights.

As war raged in Europe, racial violence was on the increase in the United States. It was encouraged, if not actually engendered by the successful motion picture, *Birth of a Nation,* directed by D.W. Griffith, based upon the racist novel, *The Clansman,* by Thomas Dixon, which romanticized the Ku Klux Klan. That year, 1915, there were almost a hundred lynchings of blacks in the United States, and the number increased the following year.

That same year, there was a mass lynching of five blacks in Lee County, Georgia, and a successful black farmer in South Carolina was mutilated and killed simply because he would not agree to a price for his cotton seed. But the most horrifying of all the year's atrocities was the torture, lynching, and burning of a young man named Jesse Washington before a mob of thousands in Waco, Texas.

There was one small victory in 1916. The NAACP lawyers, led by Moorfield Storey, managed to win a case before the U.S. Supreme Court against the "Grandfather Clauses" instituted by southern states permitting illiterate whites to vote while denying the right to illiterate blacks.

This was also an election year, and Woodrow Wilson was running for reelection. Wilson had made promises to gain black support in 1912, but he had not only refused to live up to them, he had further damaged the positions of blacks in government by instigating a policy of creating segregated offices for black and white civil servants, and he had publicly supported lynchings and black disfranchisement. Du Bois refused this time to support him. He gave the Republican candidate, Charles Evans Hughes, the opportunity to voice an opinion on civil rights, but received no answer.

For that reason Du Bois threw the support of *The Crisis* behind the Socialist Party candidate Allan L. Benson, who openly supported equal rights. Wilson was reelected, and the cause of African-Americans would deteriorate further.

Even before the United States entered World War I, the nation became paranoid about German spies. The belief was that the Germans sought out citizens who were unhappy with their government to spy for them, and the blacks in America certainly had cause to be unhappy. The only basis for this paranoia was white guilt; the witch-hunt that ensued disrupted the lives of many African-Americans while turning up no traitors. Among those harrassed by investigation was W.E.B. Du Bois.

Although Du Bois liked the German people individually, he was strongly opposed to the imperialistic German government. He supported the Allied cause wholeheartedly, though he reserved the right to criticize the racist policies of individual Allied nations, such as Belgium's actions in the Congo. While making it clear that he was a patriotic American citizen, he continued to fight inequality wherever it arose.

Inequality rose up very noticeably in the U.S. military. At first, blacks were not permitted to enlist voluntarily, but when the draft was instituted in May 1917, after the April declaration of war, they were drafted without the regard for health status or family responsibilities granted to whites. Furthermore, the draft law required separate mustering and training facilities. And in the beginning, blacks were not trained for combat but only for stevedore or manual labor jobs.

It was this last factor that was most insulting. Du Bois and the NAACP protested strongly; it was bad enough to be segregated, but at least blacks should be granted the right to fight for their country, and there should be black commissioned officers to lead them. Through the efforts of Emmett Scott (formerly Booker T. Washington's secretary), who served as black advisor to the Secretary of War, two combat divisions of African-Americans were formed—the Ninety-second and the Ninety-third. Joel Spingarn, head of the NAACP, was given appointment to the Intelligence Division of the War Department in Washington, and he was instrumental in the decision to commission 639 black officers.

The climate of racial conflict in the United States continued to worsen. In May, in Tennessee, a black man was doused with gasoline and burned alive before thousands of spectators, brought from all over by advance announcements in the press. In July, in East St. Louis, Illinois, a mob of white workers attacked and killed 125 black workers, injuring many more, then went on to destroy their homes. Growing out of union difficulties, it may have been inspired by Samuel Gompers, head of the AFL, as Du Bois claimed in *The Crisis*. To protest the riot, the NAACP led a silent parade on Fifth Avenue in New York.

The stationing of African-American troops in the South created some serious problems, adding to the incendiary mood of the country. The Twenty-fourth Infantry, black troops, were stationed in Houston, Texas. The white population there demanded they be disarmed, and then consistently insulted and abused them on the street. Finally, in September, a group of black soldiers could take no more and fought back. A riot erupted in which seventeen whites were killed. Ninety-four black soldiers were arrested, of which thirteen were sentenced to be hanged and forty-one others given life imprisonment.

Because of the worsening situation, blacks were leaving the South by the thousands, an even larger migration to the North than had occurred after the Civil War. As a result, racial hatreds also spread to the industrial northern cities, such as East St. Louis.

Du Bois was, for the first time, caught in the middle between the extremes of conservative and radical blacks, and was criticized by both sides. The period of World War I was the most successful in the life of *The Crisis*. With an annual circulation of approximately 100,000, it became fully self-supporting, including paying Du Bois' salary. He did not soften his attacks on lynching, riots, disfranchisement, or unfair treatment of blacks in the military, but he called on his fellow African-Americans to "close ranks shoulder to shoulder with our own white fellow citizens and the allied nations that are fighting for democracy." This editorial, which appeared in *The Crisis* in July of 1918, provoked an outcry from angry readers.

In December of 1918, after the Armistice, the NAACP sent Du Bois to France in hopes of having his voice heard at the Versailles Peace Conference. Woodrow Wilson was

Provoking an outcry from angry readers, Du Bois wrote in The Crisis *during World War I that African-Americans should "close ranks shoulder to shoulder with our own white citizens and the*

allied nations that are fighting for democracy." The readers wondered why blacks should fight in a war for democracy abroad when right at home their rights were nonexistant.

stressing "self determination" for all peoples in remapping the world, and he was talking of forming a League of Nations. It is clear that, once again, Du Bois believed Wilson's promises, and his hopes went beyond the problems of blacks in the United States to the problems of the suppressed black people of Africa, who had suffered long under white imperialism.

Du Bois was quickly disappointed. It was very clear that the major powers at the conference believed in self-determination for some and not for others. He was most disillusioned by England, whom he had praised in *Crisis* editorials for having an enlightened approach to its colonial empire. At the conference, England held onto its territories as tenaciously as any of the other powers. The reason expressed was that the peoples of darker color were "not ready for independence."

Frustrated that the concerns of blacks were not being considered, Du Bois organized a Pan-African Congress in Paris in February 1919, with the cooperation of the French government, the only major power willing to consider the possibility that African nations were as important as others at the Peace Conference. Fifty-seven delegates attended the first Pan-African Congress, including sixteen

Americans, twenty from the West Indies, and twelve from African nations. One of the African delegates would become a lifelong friend to Du Bois; he was Kwame Nkruma of the nation that would become Ghana.

Du Bois returned home to the United States without having achieved his goals. However, he had learned much about the involvement of black troops—both Africans and African-Americans—in the war, and had collected documents to substantiate both the valor and the mistreatment of these troops. It was clear to him that the white American officers had fought more valiantly against their own black troops than they had against the Germans. When he attempted to publish some of his findings in *The Crisis,* the United States Post Office began to deny mailing rights for the magazine's distribution, and the Department of Justice threatened to investigate Du Bois and *The Crisis* under the Espionage Act of 1917, passed by Congress for the duration of the war but enforced more stringently in the witch-hunts after the war was over.

During the war, the idealistic Du Bois had called upon his fellow African-Americans to "earn" their rights by proving their patriotism. Thousands had heeded his call. Now Du Bois called upon the United States government and the American people to show their appreciation. His call was ignored, even suppressed. The military buried the records of black valor on the battlefield, and white Americans—both North and South—turned on African-Americans with even greater violence than before. The summer of 1919 was so bloody that it became known as the "Red Summer," the worst year of white atrocities against blacks in United States history.

The NAACP did its best to try to combat the rising tide of white supremacy through peaceful and legal means. It called a national conference on lynching for May 1919 at Carnegie Hall in New York, with its principal speaker Chief Justice Charles Evans Hughes of the United States Supreme Court. This resulted in the formation of an anti-lynching crusade with two-thousand meetings around the country, raising a defense fund of $12,000 to aid blacks unjustly arrested and charged. The NAACP also launched an investigation into the causes of the Chicago Riot, as well as one into charges that the United States military had killed three-thousand Haitians during the occupation of the island.

The Dyer Anti-lynching Bill was introduced in the U.S. House of Representatives, where it passed and eventually reached the floor of the Senate. Unfortunately it was killed there by a filibuster in 1924. Numerous legal cases were instituted by the NAACP's lawyers, most of which took years to pass through the courts and most were eventually successful.

In 1920, Du Bois published an autobiography, the first of three, entitled *Darkwater.* That year he was also awarded the NAACP's Spingarn Medal. He was fifty-two years old, no longer the young "firebrand" who had launched the attack on Booker T. Washington's leadership; he had acquired knowledge and experience not just of black problems in America but throughout the world.

Du Bois often acknowledged paradoxes in his own nature. He now began to acknowledge the paradoxes in American culture as well. The political system in the United States gave lip-service to "freedom" and "equality" and "human rights" while constantly seeking ways to circumvent and corrupt these constitutional guarantees for individual selfish gain. "Machine politics" were at their height as the 1920s began; so far, Du Bois had attempted to fight this system from outside; now he encouraged African-Americans to join the system, to become a part of machine politics.

Chapter Eight

Promoting Pan-Africanism

THE WORLD HAD BEGUN to change drastically before the war, but those changes did not become especially noticeable until the 1920s. From that time on, increasingly rapid change became the norm throughout most of the world. In the United States, women had gained the right to vote; they bobbed their hair, shortened their skirts, smoked and drank in public, and danced the Charleston. The automobile and the airplane made the world seem smaller; radio and the movies made real and imagined events a part of daily lives. And in many parts of the world, governments

Du Bois doted on his daughter, Yolanda, one of the few people to whom he showed warmth. Her lavish wedding to poet Countee Cullen was one of the highlights of the Harlem Renaissance.

changed with seeming regularity, some taking extreme forms.

Socialism and communism were concepts that had been around for a long time, but now some governments were putting the concepts into practice, the most notable case being the new communist Russia. Du Bois had first encountered socialism as a concept when he was a student in Germany, and he had learned something of communism when he had moved from Atlanta to New York. He investigated both on an intellectual level and found that his own beliefs were not far from those of socialists.

However, Du Bois was much more interested in other new concepts that were less well known. He had first heard of Marcus Garvey and his Back-to-Africa movement in 1915; he thought Garvey's ideas interesting but not really viable, and he considered Garvey himself bombastic, foolhardy, and impractical. The only part of Garvey's approach he fully agreed with was the need for black domination of Africa.

What disturbed Du Bois most greatly about Garvey's movement was that it tended to become confused with his own concept of Pan-Africanism, which was a much more sound idea. Unlike most African-Americans of his time, Du Bois fully realized that the African continent was made up of many diverse nationalities and tribal backgrounds, which shared little in common except color and mutual distrust. What Pan-Africanism sought to do was to unite black leaders from the various nations through a mutual desire to achieve self-determination or independence from the white imperialistic nations that dominated them.

The second Pan-African Congress, which met in London in 1921, was one of the most successful, with thirty countries represented. It attracted worldwide attention as well as much opposition and hostility from the governments of the major powers, and it succeeded in getting the League of Nations to create an International Bureau of Labor. However, its individual members could not agree even on its basic purpose, and it was acknowledged that it was only Du Bois who held it all together.

By the time of the third Congress in 1923, the movement was already falling apart, with only thirteen countries represented. Although Du Bois would continue to try to keep it going off and on into the 1940s, it never evolved as he wanted it to, yet ultimately it had an important effect by planting the seeds that would eventually force the European nations to grant independence to their colonies.

After the 1923 Congress, Du Bois traveled to the African continent for the first time, and it was an emotionally gratifying experience for him.

Despite his growing interest in racial nationalism for Africa, Du Bois did not give up his efforts at securing equality for blacks in the United States. He continued to voice his opinions strongly in *The Crisis,* and he accepted speaking engagements as time allowed. In the early 1920s, he and the board of the NAACP were generally in agreement on most of the issues Du Bois editorialized on in *The Crisis.* They were primarily related to Pan-Africanism or to important civil rights cases such as the defense of Dr. Sweet, who had been sentenced to death for defending his home and family in the Detroit riots, and the cases resulting from the Arkansas riots and the Elaine riots.

However, the board became very upset when he launched a crusade in 1924 against white control of black education at Fisk University, which resulted in three-fourths of the Fisk students walking out. He became a hero to young black students throughout the country, who agreed with his views, and the revolts on college campuses spread from Fisk to Howard, Lincoln, and Hampton by 1927. By the time determined parents forced their children back to school, many of the colleges had instituted much needed reforms.

The 1920s were a period in which the arts in America flourished; this was true for black artists as well as white. In what has been called the "Harlem Renaissance," African-American singers, musicians, writers, and graphic artists were recognized throughout the world, among them Paul Robeson, Countee Cullen, Langston Hughes, and Jean Toomer, with whom Du Bois became friends. In 1924 he published a new book, *The Gift of Black Folk,* and began working on a second novel, *Dark Princess,* which was published in 1928. For two years in the early 1920s, he helped edit a magazine for African-American children, *Brownie's Book.* In 1926 and 1927, he helped organize the Krigwa Players Little Theater and the Crisis Book Club, and he began to award annual Du Bois literary prizes.

This was also a period for the flowering of intellectual thought and liberal ideas. Many of the intellectuals and artists of the time flirted at least briefly with socialism or even communism. Most never joined the Communist Party, but were what would later come to be termed "fellow travelers." Some traveled to Russia to see what the new communist state was like, and in at least a few cases the trips were subsidized by anonymous donors.

Du Bois received one of these free trips in 1926, supposedly paid for by an American of Russian descent, whose name was not even known to Du Bois. He spent two months touring Leningrad, Moscow, Nijni Novgorod, Kiev, and Odessa, and he was very impressed by the changes effected by communism in such a short time. He returned to the United States proclaiming, "I may be partially deceived and half-informed but if what I have seen with my own eyes and heard with my ears in Russia is Bolshevism, I am a Bolshevik." He even rationalized the restrictions on dissent as being necessary until the United States, England, and the other western powers ceased their attacks on the Russian system.

Even though Du Bois expressed admiration for the communist achievements in Russia, he did not join the Communist Party, and he did not support Communist candidates in the United States. His stance in relation to communism appears to have been like many of his public statements and writings—deliberately calculated to shock, in the hopes of making people think for themselves.

A powerful orator, Du Bois took to podiums across the nation to denounce his former friend, Booker T. Washington, whom Du Bois thought was selling out the blacks of America.

Du Bois' problem throughout most of his life was that he genuinely believed in the American system of democracy as it had been originally established. Like all African-Americans and most of the white laboring class, he was frustrated by an unwritten clause that excluded them from the guarantees of the Bill of Rights. In the 1920s and 1930s, many of these disenchanted Americans turned to concepts of socialism and communism for hope. Those with established wealth and power recognized that these concepts were a threat to their positions and they feared what might happen if masses of Americans were permitted to think for themselves.

From this fear was born the anti-communist movement in the 1920s, a vigilante group not unlike the Ku Klux Klan that would by the 1950s wield more power even than the United States government itself, demanding—and usually getting—adherence to their own concept of "Americanism" in preference to the U.S. Constitution and Bill of Rights.

It would be in this growing battle between "Americanism" and the original concepts of the founding fathers that Du Bois' courage and integrity would be tested, and his strength and heroism would be evoked. He was an unlikely candidate to be a hero—vain, self-centered, insecure, arrogant and overbearing, even snobbish. However, he had other qualities that people rarely noticed: he had a brilliant mind and tremendous knowledge; he was sensitive and perceptive; he believed in truth and honesty even when it hurt; he was an idealist who thought the American system could be made to work; and he was stubborn.

The Civil War had not been a war to end slavery; rather it had been a conflict between two different forms of slavery—the outright ownership of workers in the South and the industrial peonage system in the North. Industrialism, with its much more subtle form of unfairness, had won. Labor leaders rightly perceived that the only means they had to combat this unfairness was to unite workers into a monopoly as powerful as capital itself. The concept was valid; the practice of uniting some and excluding others—such as Jews, Italians, and African-Americans—was foolish. When union workers went on strike, naturally those excluded from membership would become willing strike-breakers, and management would welcome the conflict.

The National Urban League, an organization that Booker T. Washington had helped found, took up the battle, setting out a program of deliberate strike-breaking by blacks.

On another front, a new young radical black leader, A. Philip Randolph, began to organize unions comprised principally of African-American members. In 1925, this organization started a fight with the powerful Pullman Company that resulted in the formation of the Brotherhood of Sleeping Car Porters.

In 1917, at age twenty-eight, Randolph had begun to assume leadership of the younger generation of African-Americans, when he had founded a magazine called *The Messenger* as a part of his attempts to unionize shipyard workers in Virginia during World War I. He was an outspoken advocate of socialism, and his approach was more radical than that of Du Bois, whom he and his followers considered as accommodationist as Booker T. Washington had been.

Turning sixty in 1928, Du Bois found himself in a difficult position. Differences between him and the NAACP board were again beginning to surface because they considered his views too radical, and they were again having to subsidize *The Crisis* because of dwindling circulation. At the same time, Du Bois was under attack from the younger generation for being too conservative.

Du Bois was hardly a conservative, and the only validity to a charge of "accommodationism" was in the pragmatic approach he advocated toward machine politics, an approach he had mixed feelings about. In the 1924 presidential election he had supported Bob LaFollette and the Progressive Party. In 1928, because of the racist appeals launched by both the Democratic and Republican Parties, he advocated voting for any third-party candidate in protest. However, in state and local elections, he gave his support to any candidate who would seek out and reward the support of African-Americans. In 1928, this meant that he supported the Republican machine in Chicago because it sent Oscar DePriest to Congress, the first black in almost a generation and the first ever from the North.

In 1928, Du Bois and Nina experienced one of the rites of passage of middle age, the marriage of their daughter Yolande. The wedding was one of the most important social events of Harlem in the 1920s. Twenty-eight-year-old Yolande, after studying in London and at Fisk University, was marrying the well-known poet Countee Cullen. The wedding was large and formal, and the reception was lavish, attended by the most prominent African-American writers, artists, and intellectuals of the time. (Langston Hughes was one of the ushers.)

Chapter Nine

Years in Eclipse

IN ITS EARLY YEARS the NAACP was controlled by its board. W.E.B. Du Bois had the unique distinction of being both a board member and a hired employee. As the organization achieved success and grew, it was necessary to hire other employees, the most important being the Executive Secretary. The NAACP's first Executive Secretary was John R. Shillady, who held the position from January 1918 until May 1920. The second was James Weldon Johnson, who had the soul of a poet, the manner of a diplomat, and the strength and determination of a general. He

Walter White, who became head of the NAACP in 1931, was both self-centered and egotistical. He made life unbearable for the entire staff, including Du Bois.

was responsible for turning the NAACP into a smooth-running operation staffed entirely by blacks, and he somehow managed to get along with everyone, including Du Bois.

When he resigned in 1931, he was replaced by Walter White, a short, dapper man who had been Johnson's assistant since 1917, and whose efforts for the past two years at undermining his superior had been the primary reason for Johnson's resignation. Two years before White's appointment, at White's urging, the NAACP board had decided to make the Executive Secretary the executive officer in charge of all operations, which had been no problem while Johnson still held the position. However, White was self-centered and egotistical, and he wielded his newly acquired power ruthlessly.

During White's first year he ran roughshod over the entire hired staff of the NAACP, making the lives of everyone unbearable. The staff, in a group, approached Du Bois and asked him, as senior staff member and as a member of the board, to appeal to the board to intercede. Du Bois drafted a petition requesting White's removal and asked the entire staff to sign it; all did, including White's newly hired assistant, Roy Wilkins.

The board, including chairman Joel

Spingarn, considered the complaints excessive. After a contrite White apologized and promised to change his ways, the board asked all of the signers to withdraw their signatures. All did, except Du Bois.

Du Bois and White feuded face to face in the halls of the NAACP office and in the board meetings, but Du Bois managed to hold his own until January of 1934, when he published an article in *The Crisis* advocating what he called "nondiscriminatory segregation" as a solution to some African-American problems. What he was attempting to say was not as offensive as his choice of terminology. Most people, including the board of the NAACP, thought he was advocating and approving of racial segregation, but that was not what he was proposing at all. He was suggesting that, without giving up claims for equal rights, blacks should join together, separate from whites, to establish businesses and industries that would advance the race economically.

Walter White and the NAACP board were outraged by his proposal. Not only was segregation in any form anathema to their purpose, they had determined that African-American economic advancement was beyond the scope of the organization.

In April the board met in order to reaffirm

publicly its opposition to segregation in any form, and immediately afterward Du Bois wrote an editorial in *The Crisis* criticizing Walter White, as well as the concept of a board hiring an employee who could make and define policy for the organization. On May 21, the board again met and unanimously voted to support White, to reaffirm his power over every facet of the NAACP, and to forbid Du Bois to use the pages of *The Crisis* to criticize White or the position of the Executive Secretary.

This was the most serious slap in the face Du Bois had been given since his dispute with Villard in the early days of the NAACP. Among those voting to rebuke him were Joel Spingarn and Mary White Ovington, his staunch friends and allies for over twenty years. He responded by rising to his feet and resigning "to take effect immediately."

Du Bois was sixty-six years old, an age when many choose to retire, but he had no intention of doing so. For one thing, he had never saved money for retirement, but more importantly he did not feel it was time for him to stop thinking, speaking, and acting.

And he had a job offer that had been open to him since 1929. That year, Du Bois' old friend John Hope had become president of

Atlanta University, and he had extended an invitation for Du Bois to return there to teach, an invitation that was renewed every year when the two men got together in New York. While the six-month feud with White had been going on, Du Bois had gone to Atlanta to conduct a seminar on "Karl Marx and the Negro." Hope had urged him to accept the long-standing offer.

However, when Hope brought the matter before the board of Atlanta University, he found opposition, primarily from Florence Read, the white president of Spelman College, the new women's institution allied to Atlanta. Spelman was funded by the Rockefellers, and Read was their personal representative at Atlanta. Her fears—and presumably that of the Rockefellers—was that Du Bois was too radical. When Hope persisted in his desire to have Du Bois as head of Atlanta's sociology department, Read reluctantly gave in.

Du Bois began teaching classes at Atlanta in the fall of 1934, and he found Florence Read attempting to stymie everything he sought to achieve, from his attempts to reestablish the Negro Studies Program to his desire to publish a journal, which he intended to call *Phylon*.

Du Bois believed that the stress of being caught between him and Florence Read con-

At the age of seventy-six Du Bois was fired by the Atlanta University Board of Trustees. John D. Rockefeller, above, a heavy contributor to the school, backed the trustees.

tributed toward Hope's early death. Certainly it was untimely, coming in 1936, after Du Bois had been at Atlanta only two years.

Du Bois did have more time to write in Atlanta. His last book had been *Africa—Its Place in Modern History* in 1930. Now he was able to complete one of his best works, *Black Reconstruction in the South,* published in 1935, as well as to contribute numerous articles to magazines. Many of these proceeded to develop his idea of "nondiscriminatory segregation," which he had begun in his last months with *The Crisis.* In an article for the *Journal of Negro Education,* he argued for separate colored schools; one in the Pittsburgh *Courier* called African-Americans "a nation within a nation." In others he returned to his emphasis on a "Talented Tenth," whom he called upon to lead the masses of blacks in developing a "closed economic circle" for racial progress. He also began work on another book, *Black Folk Then and Now,* which would be published in 1939.

However, in the mid-1930s, Du Bois' attention was directed to another earlier concern: the possibility of a worldwide conflict based upon race. The prospect of war loomed again in Europe with the establishment of fascist and national socialist governments in Spain,

Italy, Germany, and Japan. The first sign of
conflict confirmed predictions Du Bois had
been making since before World War I: it was
an imperialistic attack launched by Mussolini's
Italy on Ethiopia, the most successful of self-
ruled African nations. Haile Selassie's poorly
equipped, antiquated army fought valiantly
against the power and might of modern tanks
and airplanes, but ultimately capitulated.

The years of depression and a second world
war were difficult ones for intellectuals to in-
terpret while the complex events were happening. This was especially difficult for Du Bois
because he tried to define everything through
his concept of racial motivations, rather than
perceiving that racism was merely one of the
incidentals that would apply when convenient
to the deeper underlying motivation of human
selfishness and greed.

His inabililty to grasp what was happening
is not to his discredit. Few people at the time,
or after, were able to avoid the confusion of
economic, political, governmental, and
religious systems that had been developed over
centuries and had been dumped into the twentieth century, stirred, and loosely mixed.

In hopes of better understanding what was
happening, Du Bois in 1936 and 1937 traveled
to Europe and Asia, spending much of his time

in Russia, Germany, and Japan. He generally approved of the Russian system because he saw no evidence of racism or of imperialism. However, it was Japan that he had great praise for, not because he agreed with the political or social system but merely because the Japanese were "colored" and therefore they presented hope for all non-white races. He saw Japanese imperialism as justified in order to free the colored races from white European and American imperialism.

As far as the political changes taking place in the United States were concerned, Du Bois had mixed feelings. He had been opposed to Franklin D. Roosevelt in the 1932 election because of Roosevelt's involvement in the military occupation of Haiti in 1915, but he observed the establishment of Roosevelt's New Deal with a relatively objective eye. It was not entirely unlike what was happening in other countries. In the 1920s, unrestrained capitalism had led to a worldwide economic disaster. In the 1930s, to recover from the disaster, governments took economic control of their nations, in some cases nationalizing businesses and industries, in others instituting socialist economic policies, and in some using a combination of the two. Initially, Du Bois considered Roosevelt's approach to be fascistic,

In 1912, Du Bois decided to back Theodore Roosevelt (shown here) and his Progressive Party movement that was designed to remove impedimants to individual freedom and development.

which he felt was positive because it would ultimately fail and force the United States to turn to socialism. Later he grudgingly admitted that the New Deal had brought some economic improvements for African-Americans, and he supported Roosevelt.

As World War II began to unfold, Du Bois realized that he had been wrong in virtually all of his assessments of what was happening, but he never appears to have understood why. It was probably his greatest failing that he could not comprehend the reasons behind his mistakes in judgment. Perhaps the most valid criticism of Du Bois was that he always viewed the world by looking inside himself, personalizing events and the actions of others. This was an acceptable approach for an artist or a writer, which was what he was best equipped to be, but it was a disastrous approach for a social or political leader, which is a role he assumed and even coveted.

In 1941, Du Bois continued to have only praise for the Japanese, while pleading for U.S. non-intervention in the war in Europe, but after the attack on Pearl Harbor in December, he wrote a powerful appeal to African-Americans to "close ranks" to support their country, as he had done in World War I.

During the late 1930s and the early 1940s,

Du Bois' leadership was eclipsed by younger African-Americans, most prominently A. Philip Randolph, who was making great strides in the labor movement. The CIO, organized as the Committee of Industrial Organizations in 1935 and formally constituted as the Congress of Industrial Organizations in 1938 under the leadership of John L. Lewis, was much more open to black participation than the AFL. By the time the AFL and CIO would merge in 1955, Randolph's position was such that he would be named vice president of the combined union of sixteen-million members.

During this time, Du Bois devoted most of his energy to teaching at Atlanta, writing, and improving educational opportunities for African-Americans. In 1940, at the age of seventy-two, he published his second autobiography, *Dusk of Dawn*. Even with his limited set of goals, he met resistance. In 1937, Atlanta University had hired Rufus Clement as president, replacing John Hope. Clement was not sympathetic toward Du Bois, allying himself closely with Florence Read. However, by 1940, Du Bois managed to found his journal *Phylon*, and with the aid of the Carnegie Foundation he was able to organize the first Phylon Conference in 1941 to study problems of black higher education in the United States.

It took Du Bois two years to organize, but he managed to call together an Atlanta University Conference in April of 1943 to study the Negro Land-Grand Colleges and to coordinate a program of cooperative social studies. It was highly successful, and the leaders attending agreed to hold a second conference in 1944. It would not take place.

Rufus Clement and Florence Read decided it was time for Du Bois to be "retired." He was expressing views in *Phylon* that they disagreed with. At the meeting of the board of Atlanta University in 1944, Florence Read moved that Du Bois retire from his teaching position and head of the sociology department, and Clement seconded the motion. The board, assuming this had been discussed with Du Bois, who was now seventy-six years old, voted him out of a job, retiring him without a pension.

What was in essence a firing came as a shock to Du Bois. He fought back, protesting that his "retirement" should have been discussed with him before being voted on. As a compromise the board voted to give Du Bois a pension of $1800 a year for five years and $1200 a year thereafter.

Du Bois accepted, but he wasn't about to retire. He had many good years left.

Chapter Ten

In Battle
for
Peace

D U BOIS PROBABLY COULD not have
sat back, relaxed, and peacefully enjoyed old-
age retirement even if he had wanted to. As
a young man, he had set the pattern for his
life, a pattern of striving to change the world,
and it was not a pattern he could change now.
He did not have to go in search of a job. As
soon as his "retirement" was made public, the
offers began to come in. Teaching positions
were available to him at Howard University,
Fisk University, and North Carolina College
for Negroes.

The most surprising job offer he was made,

*Du Bois near the time he was forced to leave Atlanta University
at the age of seventy-six. He would continue to be a force in
the political arena for another decade.*

and the one he accepted, was to return to the NAACP as Director of Special Research, with a special assignment to direct work on the Committee to Present the Cause of the Negro at the Next Peace Conference. It was a position that was ideally suited to Du Bois, because it focused on two of the most important causes he was concerned with—peace and the advancement of blacks throughout the world.

He was approached by two of the NAACP's board members, Louis Wright and Arthur Spingarn, whose brother Joel had died in July of 1939, but they insisted that the job offer had been suggested by Walter White, Du Bois' old enemy, who was still Executive Director. Du Bois set forth his terms for acceptance, which included a salary of $5000 a year, the freedom to write for himself, an office for him, and an office for a secretary. Wright and Spingarn agreed to the terms.

As it turned out, Walter White had no intention of meeting these terms, and his power had become so entrenched in the organization during the ten years of Du Bois' absence that he was a virtual dictator. Only the legal department, headed by Arthur Spingarn and Thurgood Marshall, which had a separate budget and separate offices, was free of White's domination. White expected Du Bois to serve as his personal ghost writer and to occupy a small cubbyhole office where he could keep his eye on the vocal old man.

The first serious problem between Du Bois and White arose in 1945. While White was in Asia, surveying the military front, the board appointed Du Bois to serve as the NAACP consultant to the San Francisco Conference organizing the United Nations. Since this was linked to the Peace Conference, a part of the job he had been hired for, Du Bois made preparations to attend. He wrote proposals for statutes for the U.N. Charter guaranteeing the rights of minorities. Just before the conference, White returned to New York, took the position for himself without consulting the board, and reduced Du Bois to his assistant. In San Francisco, White presented the proposed statutes himself.

White did not interfere with Du Bois' participation in a fifth Pan-African Congress he called for London in October, which was attended by representatives from sixty nations, but when Senator Connally asked Du Bois to testify before the congressional Committee on the Charter of the U.N., and Du Bois accepted the request, White was outraged that he had complied without his permission. The fact that Du Bois testified as an individual, not as a representative of the NAACP, did not matter to White, who took the matter before the board in an attempt to get Du Bois fired.

By this time Du Bois had realized that he would never get the office he had been promised, so he rented offices for himself at his own expense. He also accepted personal invitations to speak and to participate in conferences, to which White objected. One of these engagements was to speak at the Southern Negro Youth Congress in Columbia, South Carolina. It clearly disturbed the NAACP Executive Secretary when in January 1946 *The New Masses,* a communist publication, honored Du Bois at its Annual Awards Dinner, and then in May appointed him a contributing editor. White even began to object to Du Bois' personal correspondence, demanding that all Du Bois' mail should come to him for censoring. Du Bois adamantly refused, maintaining that his employment did not abridge his right to free speech.

In October of 1946, Du Bois called leaders of twenty African-American organizations to meet at the Schomburg Collection of the New York Public Library to create an appeal to the United Nations to free American blacks from their quasi-colonial status as "a nation within a nation." This was to be made under the aegis of the NAACP and published in pamphlet form as *An Appeal to the World*. Six writers prepared chapters, and Du Bois wrote an introduction. When it was completed, White held up the printing of the pamphlet for several months, insisting he also had to write an introduction. Finally, he allowed it to go to press, but when the U.N. agreed to hear the petition, White insisted he would be the one to speak, not Du Bois. White traveled to Geneva for the meeting, but the U.S. delegates, Eleanor Roosevelt and Jonathan Daniels, refused to permit White to be heard.

But it was a personal memorandum from Du Bois to White, which somehow was leaked to the press, that brought the conflict between Du Bois and White to a climax. White had been using his position with the NAACP to publicly support Harry Truman for reelection in 1948, for which Truman gratefully appointed White a delegate to the United Nations Organization. However, when White caught Du Bois wearing a button supporting Henry Wallace for president, he demanded the button be removed. Du Bois wrote a vitriolic memo accusing White of selling out the cause of African-Americans for his own personal political advancement.

Du Bois insisted that he was not the one who

leaked the memo, implying that it was White who had done so. When White took the matter before the NAACP board, Du Bois was promptly fired.

His friend, Paul Robeson, immediately offered him a job as his vice chairman on the Council on African Affairs. There would be no salary, but it would give Du Bois an office. At the time the Council was organized in London in 1939, Du Bois had not been invited to join. At this point, that did not matter to Du Bois, nor did it matter that the Council was on the U.S. Attorney General's list of subversive organizations. He accepted the offer.

As with World War I, the end of World War II was followed by witch-hunts in the United States, but on a larger scale because this conflict had been even more violent and had stirred up more hatred, which could not be satisfied merely with victory. A segment of the population had to find more enemies to defeat, preferably at home. This was complicated by the fact that the United States government and its bureaucracy had grown more powerful through the New Deal and wartime—and by the fact that wartime businesses had grown dependent on weapons manufacture and they did not want to give up their government contracts.

W.E.B. Du Bois shakes hands with Nikita Khrushchev during his 1959 visit to Russia. Though not a member of the Communist Party, Du Bois agreed with many parts of its doctrine.

However, there was an entirely different reaction among another segment of the United States population, primarily artists, writers, intellectuals, and educators. Horrified by the Nazi death camps and by the United States unleashing of nuclear power at Hiroshima and Nagasaki, these people were determined that wars must stop, so they formed a movement for peace, which had to be international in scope if it was to be effective. It especially had to involve people from the two great powers that had emerged from the war—the United States and Russia—which were now facing off as adversaries.

The segment of the U.S. population that needed new enemies to feed its hate latched onto pacifists as well as communists, and they were supported by those in government and business whose power and profit were dependent upon a wartime atmosphere. Thus was born what became known as the "Cold War."

Du Bois joined the peace movement at the outset. In 1949, he was involved in a series of peace crusades in various countries, beginning with one held in March at the Waldorf Astoria Hotel in New York, hosted by Russians Dmitri Shostakovitch and Alexander Fedeyev, then going on to Paris in April for the World Congress of the Defenders of Peace, which adopted a Peace Manifesto. In August he attended the All Russian Peace Congress, but missed the American Continental Congress for World Peace in Mexico City in September because he was still in Russia.

In February 1950, Du Bois' wife Nina died, after a long illness, in Baltimore, Maryland, where she had been living with their daughter Yolande since 1934, when Yolande was divorced from Countee Cullen. The Du Bois marriage had not been a happy one, but they had made adjustments and compromises to avoid divorce themselves. Nina had wanted a simple family life and was unable to share in Du Bois' intellectual and political pursuits. Du Bois had found the intellectual companionship he needed with a young African-American writer named Shirley Graham, who from time to time had worked as his secretary.

In May of 1950, the Council on African Affairs produced a Concert of Negro Composers at Town Hall in New York, intending it as an annual fund-raising event. It was a critical success and very well attended, but it cost more to produce than the organization made from ticket sales. As a result, the Council could no longer afford to pay Du Bois' office rent. Du Bois offered to pay the rent himself, but the Council came up with another fund-raising idea—an eighty-third-birthday party for Du Bois in 1951.

Du Bois agreed to this, but meanwhile he had accepted another voluntary position, Chairman of the Peace Information Center, which had opened an office in New York. The objective of this organization was to obtain American signatures to the "Stockholm Appeal," a petition to ban the use of atomic weapons that was initiated at the World Partisans for Peace meeting in Stockholm, Sweden, in March 1950. In both of these organizations, Du Bois frequently found himself in meetings with a former United States Assistant Attorney General, O. John Rogge, who had become a leader in the international peace movement and who appeared to espouse communist views.

Although there was no official United States government objection to this petition immediately, the House Committee on Un-American Activities labeled it "communist chicanery." It was not until July 12, eleven days after the first U.S. troops landed in Korea, beginning involvement in the Korean War, that official objections began, with Secretary of State Dean Acheson issuing a broadside attacking the Peace Information Center as a communist-front organization and demanding that it cease to circulate the petition, which by this time had over a million signatures in the U.S. In August, the Peace Information Center received a request from the Justice Department to register as the agent of a foreign power. To the board members, this request seemed ludicrous, and they ignored it.

That same month, Du Bois applied for and received a visa to attend the World Congress of the Defenders of Peace in Prague, Czechoslovakia, but with restrictions placed on his travel. While he was abroad, Du Bois received a cable from John Abt of the American Labor party asking him to run for the United States Senate. Du Bois knew he had no chance of winning the seat against Herbert H. Lehman, but felt his name on the Labor ticket might help the candidacy of Vito Marcantonio for congressman, so he agreed.

As his campaign got under way, the Department of Justice stepped up its campaign against the Peace Information Center, demanding on September 19 that the organization register as a representative of a foreign agency immediately. On October 12, Abbott Simon, Director of the Peace Information Center, issued a statement that it had no obligation to register because it had no affiliation with the World Congress of the Defenders

Shirley Graham became Du Bois' second wife. They wed on Valentine's Day, 1951, when Du Bois was eighty-two. She was a constant and faithful companion in his final years.

of Peace, as the government was charging. However, the center's board decided to disband to avoid further problems.

Du Bois and the other board members assumed that was the end of the matter. On October 24, as a part of his campaign for senator, Du Bois delivered a speech before a crowd of 17,000 in Madison Square Garden. As expected, he was not elected, but when the returns came in he was surprised that he had received less than four percent of the vote.

In January of 1951, the invitations went out for Du Bois' eighty-third-birthday party, to be held at the Essex House in New York, and Du Bois and Shirley Graham began to talk of marriage. However, all plans were to change after a Washington, D.C., grand jury, under the prompting of Attorney General J. Howard McGrath, indicted Du Bois on February 9, under the Foreign Agents Registration Act.

Fearing he would be imprisoned, Du Bois and Shirley were married in secret on February 14, and after the birthday celebration on February 23, they set out around the country to raise funds for his defense. Although the case would ultimately be thrown out of court in November, Du Bois became embittered in spirit.

This time in United States history was to

become known as "the McCarthy Era," named for the period's leading hate-mongerer, Senator Joseph McCarthy, but the government and the general population were filled with people who sought to destroy lives, careers, and the Bill of Rights to advance their own right-wing political beliefs.

After his acquittal, Du Bois was embittered but still determined to fight for his rights as a United States citizen; the United States government was just as determined to deny those rights. From 1952 through 1959, he would be continually harassed by the FBI, the police, and various government agencies. In February of 1952, he applied for a visa to travel to Brazil for a conference, and it was denied. Shortly afterward, he flew to Toronto, where no passport was required, to attend a Canadian peace conference; and when he arrived, he was met by U.S. officials at the airport, who put him on a plane back to the United States. In 1953, when he applied for a passport, he was asked to sign a loyalty oath. He refused, maintaining that no political statement was required. The passport was denied.

For a time Du Bois accepted defeat, concentrating his energy on the writing of a trilogy of novels. The first, *The Ordeal of Mansart,* was published in 1957; the second, *Mansart*

Du Bois with Mao Tse-tung on a visit to China in 1959. After the China visit the United States Department of State took away his passport whereupon he moved to Ghana.

Builds a School, in 1959; and the third, *An ABC of Color,* in 1963. However, in 1957, after Ghana was granted its independence from Great Britain, his old friend Kwame Nkruma, who had been the territorial Prime Minister since 1952 and would be the new nation's first president in 1960, invited Du Bois to attend the independence celebration. He again applied for a passport, and again was denied because he refused to state that he had never been a member of the Communist Party.

Now approaching ninety, Du Bois must have felt the irony in the fact that his own personal liberties were being curtailed while the government was taking positive steps toward granting African-Americans the equal rights he had fought for most of his life. In 1954, the U.S. Supreme Court decided in *Brown vs the Board of Education of Topeka* that school segregation was illegal, and it urged "all deliberate speed" in desegregation. The case had been led by attorney Thurgood Marshall of the NAACP. On December 5, 1955, a young minister named Martin Luther King, Jr., led a bus boycott in Montgomery, Alabama, in response to mistreatment of an elderly black lady named Rosa Parks; it lasted a year, ending only when the Supreme Court ordered desegregation of local transportation.

In some parts of the United States, the opening of schools and colleges to blacks was met with resistance, sometimes with violence, but even the U.S. Congress saw the tide of justice, on August 29, 1957, passing its first Civil Rights bill since 1876.

In 1958, the Supreme Court issued a decision, ruling that the State Department had no authority to demand political statements such as loyalty oaths as a basis for issuing passports. Du Bois promptly applied for one, and it was granted. In July, he set off for a visit to the Soviet Union, staying for five months, during which time he had a personal visit with Nikita Khruschev. Then he went on to a tour of Red China, where he celebrated his ninety-first birthday with Mao Tse-Tung, returning to the United States in April of 1959. Immediately, the U.S. State Department revoked his passport for visiting China, a banned country.

For a time it appeared that his hopes of attending the inauguration of Kwame Nkruma as first president of Ghana would be foiled. Du Bois was now feeling his age; in 1960 his daughter Yolande died of a heart attack; his grandson, Du Bois Williams, child of Yolande by her second husband, Arnett Williams, was twenty-eight years old. Du Bois was almost, but not quite, resigned to the end of his life, still fighting. However, Nkruma used his influence to have Du Bois' passport reinstated.

In July he traveled to Accra, Ghana, to attend the inauguration. While he was there, Nkruma asked him to move to Ghana and finally compile his *Encyclopedia Africana,* which had been one of Du Bois' great dreams. He returned home to the United States and took care of all the business necessary for an extended move.

On October 1, 1961, before taking his departure from the United States, Du Bois joined the Communist Party as an act of defiance. He was not, and never had been, a communist, but the futile act was meant to show the stupidity of a government attempting to place discriminatory labels on something as elusive as human conscience. The point was lost on the U.S. State Department.

When, in 1963, Du Bois' passport expired, he applied to the U.S. Consul in Accra for it to be renewed, but it was denied because Du Bois was "a communist." He officially gave up his U.S. citizenship and asked to become a citizen of Ghana. President Kwame Nkruma welcomed his decision, naming him "the first citizen of Africa" and helped him celebrate his ninety-fifth birthday on February 23, his last.

A succession of black leaders passed along the role of "Moses" from one generation to the next, beginning with Frederick Douglass to Booker T. Washington to Du Bois and King.

On August 27, 1963, W.E.B. Du Bois suddenly became ill in Accra. Before he died, President Nkruma managed to rush to his side to be with him.

News of his death spread through the crowd of two-hundred-thousand marchers gathered in Washington on August 28, and many were saddened, but the news was overshadowed by words the new, young leader, Martin Luther King, Jr., declaimed before the crowds, announcing, "I have a dream!" He likened himself to Moses, questioning whether he would see the promised land, and indeed he was the African-American Moses of the 1960s. There had been a succession of black leaders who had dreamed his dream, each handing the role of Moses to the next generation—from Frederick Douglass to Booker T. Washington to W.E.B. Du Bois to A. Philip Randolph and finally to King.

In Accra, Du Bois was given a state funeral and buried in a prominent place outside the Ghanian Government House. The United States was the only major nation not to send an official representative to the funeral.

In 1968, the hundredth anniversary of Du Bois' birth, his third and last autobiography was published, *The Autobiography of W.E.B. Du Bois*.

After he became a citizen of that country, the University of Ghana awarded Du Bois an honorary degree. President Kwame Nkruma named him "the first citizen of Africa."

INDEX